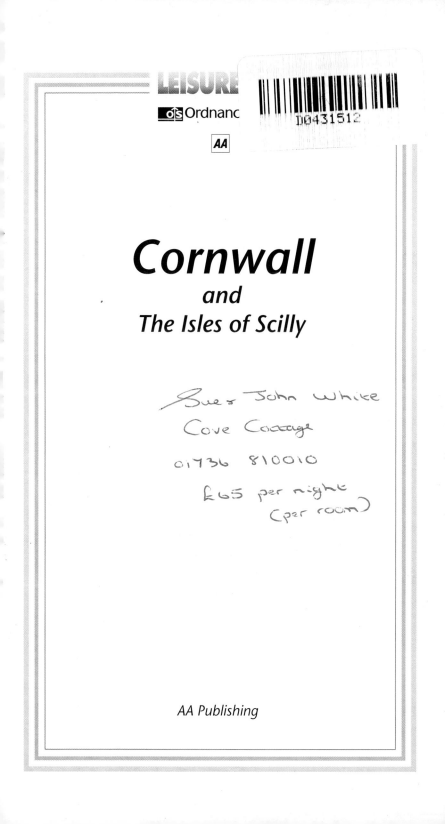

LEISURE

OS Ordnanc

*AA*

D0431512

# *Cornwall*
## *and*
### *The Isles of Scilly*

*Sue & John White*
*Cove Cottage*
*01736 810010*
*£65 per night*
*(per room)*

*AA Publishing*

Author: Des Hannigan

Page layout: Stuart Perry

First edition published 1996
by Ordnance Survey and
AA Publishing.
Reprinted 1996, 1997, 1998.
Second edition 1999.
Ordnance Survey, Romsey Road,
Southampton SO16 4GU.

AA Publishing, a trading name of
Automobile Association
Developments Limited, whose
registered office is Norfolk House,
Priestley Road, Basingstoke,
Hampshire RG24 9NY. Registered
Number 1878835.

Gazetteer map references are taken
from the National Grid and can be
used in conjunction with AA and
Ordnance Survey maps and atlases.
Places featured in this guide will
not necessarily be found on the
maps at the back of the book.

A CIP catalogue record for this
book is available from the British
Library.

ISBN 07495 2052 3

Colour reproduction by L C Repro

Printed and bound by G. Canale &
C. s.p.a., Torino, Italy

The contents of this book are
believed correct at the time of
printing. Nevertheless, the
publishers cannot accept
responsibility for errors or
omissions, or for changes in
details given in this guide or for the
consequences of any reliance on
the information provided by the
same. We have tried to ensure
accuracy in this guide, but things
do change and we would be
grateful if readers would advise us
of any inaccuracies they may
encounter.

# Contents

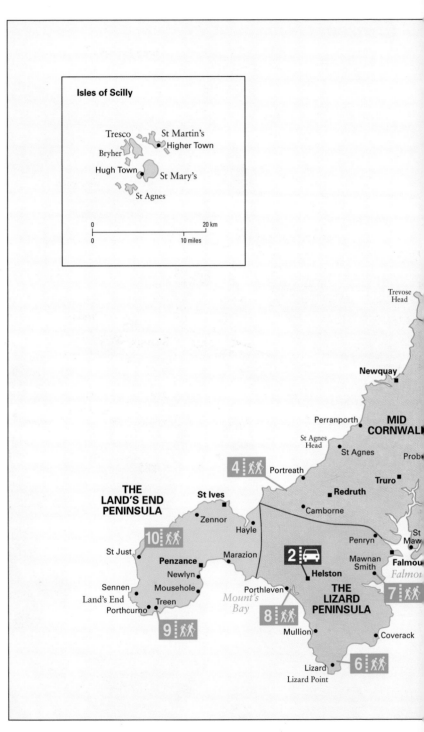

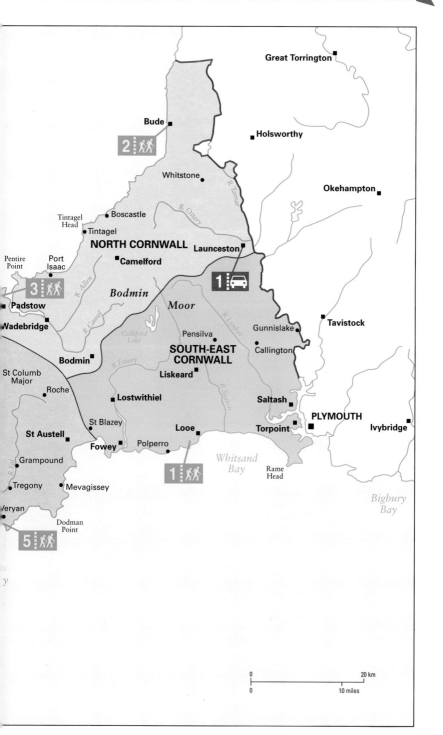

# Introducing
# Cornwall and the Isles of Scilly

## A FLAVOUR OF CORNWALL

Cornwall, a long, dwindling peninsula which draws the visitor on to where England finally gives way to the Atlantic, is a county of dramatic, yet contrasting coastlines. The invigorating north is where dark echoing cliffs lead on to Land's End. The south is more passive and green, with a succession of deep bays between bold promontories. It is a coastline of towns and fishing villages famous for their narrow, cobbled streets and colourful harbours.

Inland are the granite heights of Bodmin Moor, a maze of quiet lanes, tranquil villages, and the larger towns of rural Cornwall.

Cornwall is where hospitality is of the highest, a county that is reassuringly a part of Britain, but with the style, the atmosphere and the excitement of another country.

The Isles of Scilly lie 28 miles off Land's End. Known as the 'Sunshine Islands', they offer golden beaches, crystal-clear sea, and quiet green corners inland.

RICHARD TREVITHICK
*A Camborne man and 'Father of the Locomotive', Richard Trevithick was a hero of Cornwall's Industrial Revolution*

CORNISH CUSTOMS
*Summer festivals are cheerfully celebrated in traditional style throughout Cornwall, from Padstow to Helston*

PISKIES
*Cornish piskies can be blamed for any mischief, and if you're wandering in a dazed fashion, you may be 'piskie-led'*

SEA SHELLS
*You're never far from the sea, and a souvenir shell held to the ear will recall the sound of Cornish waves*

SIR JOHN BETJEMAN
*Sir John Betjeman, who holidayed happily near Polzeath, is one of the many writers to evoke the area*

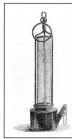

**SIR HUMPHRY DAVY AND HIS LAMP**
Sir Humphry Davy, the scientist famous for his invention of the miners' safety lamp, was born in Penzance in 1778

**CORNISH LIFEBOATS**
Heroic tales of rescue at sea are to be heard all around the Cornish coastline

**RARE CORNISH HEATHER**
A distinctive flora awaits discovery, both on the coast and inland, including rare orchids and the Cornish Heath

**CORNISH SEABIRDS**
Seabirds breed all along the coastline, and are noisy – and not always welcome – visitors inland

## ESSENTIAL CORNWALL

If your time in Cornwall is limited try not to miss the best of the county:

**Experience** the essence of Cornwall portrayed through great paintings at the Tate Gallery St Ives... **Enjoy** a delicious cream tea... **Visit** Cotehele, a beautiful Tudor house which lies amidst deep woods in elegant seclusion... **Discover** the magnificent Lost Gardens of Heligan, the largest garden reclamation project in Europe... **Drive** along the B3306 coast road between St Ives and St Just, one of the finest scenic routes in England... **Walk** the cliff tops at Land's End, the quieter reaches of the Helford Estuary or the lonely heights of Bodmin Moor... **Visit** the charming fishing village of Mevagissey (be prepared for lively crowds during the busy holiday periods)... **Watch** the surfers at Newquay... **Cruise** up the River Fal, or take a fishing trip from Falmouth... **Treat** yourself to the taste of Cornwall at Padstow's celebrated Seafood Restaurant.

**CORNISH PASTIES**
The eminently portable Cornish pasty has been called an early convenience food, and is one of many local delicacies

**BARBARA HEPWORTH**
The work of sculptress Barbara Hepworth is celebrated in her adopted home town of St Ives

## TEN BEST PLACES

Antony House
Mount Edgcumbe Country Park
Cothele
Heligan Gardens
Lanhydrock
Trerice
Truro Cathedral
Trelissick
St Michael's Mount
Tate Gallery St Ives

**CORNISH SEALS**
Curious seals can observe the tourists more closely at Gweek's National Seal Sanctuary

# A Weekend in Cornwall

For many people a weekend break or a long weekend is a popular way of spending their leisure time.

These four pages offer a loosely planned itinerary designed to ensure that you make the most of your time and see and enjoy the very best the area has to offer.

Options for wet weather and children are given where possible.

Places with Gazetteer entries are in **bold**.

## Friday Night

Stay in **St Ives** at The Garrack, a small hotel situated high above the town in secluded surroundings. Enjoy views of the spectacular coastal scenery along with the welcoming atmosphere and wonderful food.

Wander around the harbour area at St Ives in the evening.

## Saturday Morning

Stroll through attractive Fore Street, and on through the narrow, cobbled streets of St Ives with their numerous galleries and craft workshops. Visit the Tate Gallery and the Barbara Hepworth Gallery and Sculpture Garden.

St Ives' magnificent beaches are an alternative attraction when the weather is fine.

Leave St Ives on the B3306 north coast road, via **Zennor** and **Gurnard's Head**, through the glorious scenery of the Land's End Peninsula. Just before Morvah, at Trevowhan, turn left to visit the remains of a prehistoric burial chamber at Lanyon Quoit.

*Explore the narrow lanes of old St Ives, above*

*The Tate Gallery, left, is a fine showcase for modern art*

*Cross by ferry or the causeway from Marazion to visit magical St Michael's Mount, above*

*Towns such as Helston offer a friendly welcome, right*

*Inland, discover Cornwall's peaceful woods and rivers, below*

Alternatively, remain on the B3306 and continue to **Land's End** where there are exhibitions and wet weather attractions for everyone.

## Saturday Lunch

Head for **Marazion** via the A30 and the A394, where a good place for lunch, in summer, is the Mount Haven Hotel at the eastern end of the town. There are splendid views out across Mount's Bay and to **St Michael's Mount**.

## Saturday Afternoon

Reach St Michael's Mount, either on foot across the cobbled causeway or by ferry boat if the tide is in. The Mount is in the care of the National Trust and both house and gardens are delightful. For children, the world of castles and cannons in such a wonderful maritime setting is irresistible.

Take the A394 to **Helston** and on through Gweek to Mawnan Smith. This is Cornwall's other landscape, a world of wooded creeks and quiet lanes, a delightful contrast to the rugged seascapes of St Ives and the wild moorland of the Land's End Peninsula.

## Saturday Night

Stay at the Budock Vean Hotel on the banks of the Helford River near Mawnan Smith. Set amidst beautiful gardens and parkland with a private foreshore to the Helford, the hotel includes a golf course among its leisure facilities.

# A Weekend in Cornwall: Day Two

Your second and final day offers a choice of expeditions, on foot, through the Helford area followed by a visit to one of Cornwall's loveliest gardens, Glendurgan. If the weather is bad, Falmouth, only a short distance away, has numerous wet weather attractions.

## Sunday Morning

If it is wet drive north to **Falmouth**.

The best way to enjoy the beauties of the **Helford** area is on foot. The northern shore of the estuary, and its adjoining coastline, provides splendid walking (See Walk on page 86). Alternatively a ferry trip from Helford Passage takes you to Helford village. From here you can walk to Frenchman's Creek, made famous by Daphne du Maurier.

Helford can also be reached by a short drive round the end of the Helford River (See Car Tour on page 84). The route passes through Gweek where a visit to the Seal Sanctuary will delight children and adults alike.

## Sunday Lunch

For lunch, if you decide on a walk round the Mawnan Smith coast, then it might be best to take a picnic. If you cross to Helford, then try the 17th-century Shipwright Arms. This friendly pub, in a delightful riverside setting, provides a good selection of tasty meals.

*Frenchman's Creek inspired a tale of smugglers, left*

*At Gweek you can admire the seal life, below*

### Sunday Afternoon

Visit the National Trust's Glendurgan Garden, a valley garden of great beauty. Children will love the laurel maze. The adjacent Trebah Garden, which lies in a steep-sided valley, is also delightful.

Don't forget to make time for a delicious cream tea to round off your weekend tour of Cornwall at its best.

*Enjoy the rhododendrons in bloom at Glendurgan Garden, above*

*The lush semi-tropical gardens at Trebah offer spectacular vistas, right*

*Visit the attractive villages along the Helford River, left*

# South-east Cornwall: Liskeard, Looe and Fowey

South-east Cornwall is where singing rivers run south from the high ground of Bodmin Moor through woods and well-farmed fields to reach one of the loveliest coastlines in England. It is a coast that begins within sight of Plymouth at the peaceful Rame Peninsula, from where it runs west past spacious beaches to the port of Looe and the fishing village of Polperro. Further west the coastline traces its intricate way in and out of tiny coves and around handsome headlands as far as Fowey's graceful river and town. Between the granite country of the high moor and the coast, are the bustling market towns of Liskeard and Lostwithiel and the quiet villages of an older Cornwall.

## THE CORNISH LANGUAGE

Cornish was a branch of the Celtic languages that still survive in Ireland, Wales, Scotland and Brittany, and was similar to the latter. In the 16th century Cornwall was denied its own Cornish prayer book and bible – a fatal blow to the language. The Mousehole fishwife Dolly Pentreath (died 1777) was thought to have been the 'last Cornish speaker'. But Dolly, who also spoke English, may take second place to John Davey of Zennor (died 1891) whose main language was English, but could converse in basic Cornish. Cornish is now being successfully revived by academics and enthusiasts.

*Georgian perfection at Antony House*

## ANTONY HOUSE  Map ref SX4256

Antony House, home of the Carew family for generations, stands in handsome grounds on the banks of the Lynher River near Torpoint. The original Tudor house was pulled down in the early years of the 18th century. In its place William Carew built the finest Georgian house in Cornwall, perfectly proportioned with granite stonework lending power and weight. Facings of Pentewan stone and colonnaded wings of red brick blur the solidity without detracting from the grandness of the whole. The interiors are oak panelled and the delightful furnishings include unusual single four-poster beds. Antony House is in the care of the National Trust.

## CAWSAND AND KINGSAND  Map ref SX4350

The villages of Cawsand and Kingsand lie on the Rame
Peninsula within 3 miles (4.8km) of Plymouth; but
because the high ground of Mount Edgcumbe lies
between, there is no awareness of a large city and port
being so close. The two villages which now merge
seamlessly were once divided by the old Devon–
Cornwall border between Saxon England and the Celtic
West – look out for the old sign on Garrett Street. The
Saxons took control of both sides of the Tamar, a wise
defence against the ever present threat of attack by
Viking raiders.

For generations those born in Kingsand were recorded
as being Devon born, but today Cawsand and Kingsand
sit comfortably together in Cornwall. Cawsand has a
charming little square above its small beach and from
here you can walk along the seemingly never-ending
Garrett Street to Kingsand, through light and shade and
past a rather grand clock tower. Explore the narrow
alleyways and flights of steps that sidle to and fro above
the rocky shoreline.

Running south from Cawsand is a level walk that leads
along part of a Victorian drive, built by the Earl of
Edgcumbe. Wealthy landowners of the 18th and 19th
centuries often built such driveways through their
properties in order to show them off to their guests. The
way leads through delightful woods to Penlee Point
where there is an intriguing grotto built against the slope
of the headland. From here the graceful curve of Rame
Head can be seen to the west.

*Set in a nick of the Rame
Peninsula, Cawsand
overlooks the entrance to
Plymouth Sound*

### MOUNT EDGCUMBE COUNTRY PARK

The original house at Mount
Edgcumbe was destroyed by
an incendiary bomb during
World War II, a peripheral
victim of the massive raids on
Plymouth. It was rebuilt
during the 1950s to replicate
the original and has been
handsomely restored. The
landscaped park is an
outstanding example of an
early 18th-century park. It has
numerous engaging features
such as follies, mock temples
and Gothic ruins; and
exquisite formal gardens. The
park's woodland has a
network of paths and fallow
deer roam among the trees.
Near by is the little river port
of Cremyll from where there is
a passenger ferry to Plymouth.

*The twelve high arches of Calstock's graceful viaduct span the Tamar valley*

**KIT HILL**

The granite dome of Kit Hill rises to a height of just over 1,000 feet (305m) above the town of Callington, about 4 miles (6.4km) north west of Calstock. It stands in splendid isolation, as if torn between the granite masses of Bodmin Moor to the west and Dartmoor to the east. For centuries Kit Hill was quarried for stone and delved into for tin, copper, zinc, lead and even silver, but it is now a country park in the care of Cornwall County Council. The hill is crowned by an 80-foot (21m) chimney stack that was built in 1858 as part of the engine house of the Kithill Consols mine. The views from the summit are outstanding and there are lots of pathways around the hill, including a circular walk and a heritage trail.

**CALSTOCK**  Map ref SX4368

Calstock is Cornish, but its position is deceptive. It stands on the north bank of the meandering River Tamar (the county boundary) within an enclave of land almost surrounded by Devon.

Calstock has been a Tamar River quay since the Saxons came to Cornwall. For centuries sand and lime carried upriver on Tamar barges were used for improving the soil of surrounding farms. Tin and copper, and quarried granite from nearby Kit Hill, were transported back to Plymouth and at Calstock there was shipbuilding, paper-making and brick-making. Until the railway came to the Tamar Valley, full-masted schooners, steam-powered coasters, barges and paddle steamers all berthed at Calstock's quay.

In the 20th century, market gardening in the surrounding countryside has been a thriving business, but Calstock's great industrial days are long gone, leaving a rich heritage amidst the loveliness of the Tamar countryside. Calstock's great glory is its viaduct – built in 1906 with manufactured blocks, it is a triumph of good design and engineering. Today, the railway still links Calstock to the outer world, but it remains a Tamar river settlement and passenger boats from Plymouth still come upriver to tie up at Calstock where pubs and restaurants, shops and galleries add to the attractions.

West of Calstock is Cotehele (National Trust), a Tudor house of great beauty which lies amidst deep woods in elegant seclusion. The Tudor style of the house has been preserved virtually intact thanks to the fact that in 1533 the owner, Richard Edgcumbe, built Mount Edgcumbe House on Plymouth Sound and made that the family seat. Cotehele then became a second home. Even the furnishings at Cotehele have a rare antiquity, with intricate tapestries of Flemish design and beautifully decorated furniture.

The gardens are exquisite and date from the Victorian period, an interesting contrast with the house and its interiors, yet one that sits easily with the Tudor style. The original estate mill has been restored to working order and there is an adjoining cider press.

Cotehele was dependent on the Tamar for communications, and some of the old buildings on the nearby quay have been preserved; one is now a small museum relating to river transport and the working life of the Tamar. The restored sailing barge *Shamrock* is now moored at the quay.

### EAST BODMIN MOOR  Map ref SX2574

Cornwall's largest area of high moorland has been bisected by the A30, but the moor falls naturally into contrasting east and west sectors. The eastern side seems less wild and rugged than the undulating hills and rocky ridges of Brown Willy and Rough Tor to the west, while around the village of Minions it has all the raw beauty of wild country. The moor has been torn apart in places. The ragged, gaping hole of Cheesewring Quarry above Minions is the result of a moorland industry that was as vigorous as the copper mining that has left behind the great engine houses of the nearby Phoenix United Mine.

Cheesewring's granite was used in the building of Devonport Dockyard, Birkenhead Docks and part of Copenhagen Harbour and was included in the materials used in the Thames Embankment, Westminster and Tower Bridges and even a lighthouse in Ceylon. The quarry's name comes from the remarkable rock formation that stands at its western edge, named after its similarity to a cider press used to squeeze the 'cheese' or juice from apples. It is formed by erosion by wind and water of the weaker horizontal joints in the granite.

Close to the south-western edge of the quarry is the reconstructed cave dwelling of Daniel Gumb, an 18th-century stone cutter who built a much larger original cave dwelling here for himself and his family. Gumb was

**ANCIENT STONES**

About 2 miles (3.2km) south-west of Minions, on the roadside, is King Doniert's Stone. Inscribed in crude Latin is the legend, 'Doniert ordered this cross for the good of his soul' (the ruling elite in Cornwall used a form of dog Latin for ceremonial purposes long after the Roman occupation had ended). The adjoining cross shaft has some decoration on it. King Doniert may have been the 9th-century Cornish king Dumgarth, who is believed to have drowned in the nearby River Fowey. At Trethevy are the remains of a Neolithic tomb (quoit) of the period between 4000 to 2000 BC. An outstanding example of a chieftain's chamber tomb, its great stones are virtually intact. Originally it would have been partly covered with stones and earth but with the entrance left easily accessible for future interment of the chieftain's relatives.

*Strange formations of weathered granite adorn the heights of Bodmin Moor*

## DOZMARY POOL

Atmospheric Dozmary Pool is reached from the A30 (See Car Tour on page 46). Dozmary boils with myth and legend. The most enduring story is of the infamous Jan Tregeagle, a wonderfully nasty piece of work – actually a composite figure of several generations of Tregeagles. They were magistrates, lawyers and land stewards of the 16th, 17th and 18th centuries, and were notorious for their brutality and dishonesty. The mythological Jan Tregeagle was a disgruntled spirit, condemned by the devil to impossible tasks, such as baling out Dozmary Pool with a holed shell. These sombre waters have also been claimed as the last resting place of Excalibur.

*Old workings mark the extraction of slate, granite, china clay and even gold from the moor*

a stone cutter with considerable intellectual gifts. He was known as 'the Mountain Philosopher' and was said to be well-versed in astronomy and mathematics as well. Gumb's original cave was destroyed when Cheesewring Quarry was extended in the 1870s, but the roof of the present one is part of the original and has on its surface a carving of one of Euclid's theorems.

Bodmin Moor is much older than its industry. Close to Minions village is a cluster of early Bronze-Age (2500–1500 BC) monuments including the stone circles of the Hurlers and their adjacent standing stones. Craddock Moor to the west is peppered with burial mounds of the Bronze Age, hut circles of the Iron Age, and medieval field systems. North of Minions is Twelve Men's Moor and the chaotic rocky ridges of Kilmar Tor and Bearah Tor. Further north, a broad sweep of moorland runs through marshy ground to Fox Tor and then washes up against the asphalt boundary of the A30. To the west, the River Fowey flows from near Bolventor and the famous Jamaica Inn, through a long, shallow valley. There are great reservoirs with the characteristics of natural lakes at Colliford and Siblyback, and where the Fowey turns to the west at Draynes Bridge it pours through deep woods and moss-shrouded boulders at Golitha Falls. North of Minions, the moor drops suddenly into the deeply wooded valley of the River Lynher with peaceful hillside villages, such as North Hill. The open moorland is privately owned and although there is access, visitors are requested to treat the area with respect.

## FOWEY  Map ref SX1251

Buildings crowd out Fowey's waterfront but there is a wonderful sense of unity within the jumble of narrow streets and there is unexpected access to the harbour and quay from various points. Fowey (pronounced 'Foy') was a major port from the earliest times. Over 700 seamen from the town and its surrounding parishes took part in the Siege of Calais in 1346 when the town supplied 47 vessels compared to London's 25. In return, Fowey was attacked and burnt by the French in 1380 and in 1467. It was the Port of Cornwall in every sense and its seamen earned the title 'the Fowey Gallants'. They were outstanding sailors but were known for their arrogance and contempt for the Law, and their energies soon turned to lucrative piracy. When Edward IV took a grip on the port, Fowey turned instead to equally lucrative, but honest trade. China clay and the enterprise of the Treffry family brought prosperity, and today ocean-going ships pass upriver to Golant quays from where clay is still exported.

Fowey draws you in from the long descent of Lostwithiel Street to Trafalgar Square, then on round the Town Quay and Webb Street. The buildings crowd in from all sides and even the dark-stoned Church of St Fimbarrus with its decorated tower seems to overhang. The true face of Fowey is seen from the river or from Polruan on the opposite shore. Tall houses rise sheer from the waterfront, and when night falls in summer the boat-bobbing river is starred with lights. From the bottom of Lostwithiel Street, the Esplanade leads south west to Readymoney Cove where a small sandy beach lies below tree-shrouded St Catherine's Point.

*Boats and Fowey have always gone together*

### FOWEY FAMILIES

Cornish families had their share of the prosperity that emerged from the 15th and 16th centuries. The Rashleighs of Fowey made their money from the lucrative sea trade. They came to own most of the Gribbin Peninsula and much land round Fowey; the town's Ship Inn was once a Rashleigh town house. Menabilly, inland from Gribbin Head, was the largest of their many properties. Another great Fowey family are the Treffrys whose house at Place still dominates the town. During the reign of Richard III the Treffrys fled to Brittany to join Henry Tudor. When he became Henry VII at the Battle of Bosworth in 1485 they returned in triumph. John Treffry was knighted, their lands were restored to him and the family prospered.

*Picturesque cottages lead down to the 14th-century church at Fowey*

**FERRY EXCURSIONS**
A good way to visit Polruan from Fowey is by ferry. In summer a passenger ferry leaves from Whitehouse Quay, off the Esplanade; a winter service runs from Fowey's Town Quay. Take a bicycle on the ferry and follow the minor road east from Polruan to Lansallos and on to Polperro, or walk the coast path to Pencarrow Head and Lansallos. Coastal and river cruises also operate from the Town Quay. A car ferry at Caffamill Pill goes to Bodinnick on the opposite side of the river giving access to the beautiful coastline east of Polruan.

The Point is crowned by St Catherine's Castle, built between 1538 and 1542 as part of the chain of defences set up along the eastern and southern coasts of England by Henry VIII in response to hostility from France and the Holy Roman Empire. The castle can be reached up steep steps from the beach or by a leisurely stony track.

Driving through Fowey should be avoided at the busiest times. The main car park at the entrance to the town is well-signed from the A3082. You will find a good mix of shops lining Fowey's bustling streets, along with fine galleries, craft and antique shops. The pubs are full of a sea-going atmosphere and there are several good restaurants. The museum is in the town hall at Trafalgar Square and the Tourist Information Centre is at the far end of Fore Street.

Overlooking the town is Place, the historic home of the Treffry family. The original house was built in the troubled times of the 15th century, more as a fortress than a home, but Place was rebuilt in Regency Gothic style during the 19th century – 'Romantic baronial' may be a more apt description of such a delightfully eccentric building.

Tree-shrouded Golant lies 1½ miles (2.4km) north of Fowey and is reached from the B3269. In this charming village the small but absorbing church of St Sampson commemorates one of Cornwall's great Celtic saints.

## GRIBBIN HEAD   Map ref SW0949

West of Fowey, the smooth, green bulk of Gribbin Head (National Trust) shoulders out the western sea, preventing it from having too much influence on sheltered Fowey. The headland, always referred to as the Gribbin, is crowned with a bizarre monolith – the 84-foot (25m) Daymark tower painted in barber-shop red and white. The Daymark was erected in 1832 in order to distinguish the Gribbin from St Anthony's Head at the entrance to Falmouth Bay. The two headlands look very similar from the seaward approach and, even though Falmouth is quite a way further west from Fowey, sailors regularly mistook the Gribbin for St Anthony's Head, with catastrophic results when they sailed into the shallows of St Austell Bay instead of the deep waters of Falmouth Bay.

Just inland of the Gribbin is Menabilly, where Daphne du Maurier made her home and found inspiration for a number of her novels. In the eastern shelter of the Gribbin is Polridmouth Cove (pronounced P'ridmouth), a serene little haven with adjoining beaches and an ornamental lake.

The Gribbin can be reached on foot from a small car park at Menabilly Barton, a mile (1.6km) inland. To the west, Polkerris faces into St Austell Bay. There is a car park halfway down the tree-shaded approach, from where it is a short walk to the secluded and quietly beautiful cove. Polkerris was a busy pilchard fishing cove from Tudor times until early this century and the old sheds, known as pilchard cellars where the fish were pressed for oil, survive. The cove has a sandy beach and is sheltered at the southern end by an old stone jetty.

**DU MAURIER COUNTRY**

Cornwall's romantic image owes much to the novelist Daphne du Maurier, who, in 1926, made the Fowey area her home and her inspiration. From 1943 she was tenant of Menabilly near Gribbin Head and the house featured in *Rebecca* and *My Cousin Rachel*. The short story 'The Birds' was set amidst the lonely fields of Menabilly Barton Farm, from where it took flight via Hitchcock's fertile imagination to a celluloid California. Du Maurier immortalised Jamaica Inn on Bodmin Moor and Frenchman's Creek on the Helford River, but she best revealed her profound love for Cornwall in her non-fiction book *Vanishing Cornwall*, a perceptive critique of the erosion of old values and of the traditional landscape of her beloved county.

*The little sandy bay of Polkerris was a centre for the pilchard industry in Elizabethan times*

**THE NATIONAL TRUST IN CORNWALL**

The National Trust looks after some of the finest buildings and gardens in Cornwall, such as Lanhydrock, St Michael's Mount, Trelissick, Glendurgan and Trengwainton. The Trust also cares for over 100 miles (161km) of Cornwall's outstanding coastline including the magnificent headlands of the Rumps at Pentire, Gurnard's Head, Cape Cornwall, the Dodman and Gribbin Head. The Trust owns the summit of Rough Tor on Bodmin Moor, Zennor Hill, Loe Pool, Kynance Cove and the shores of the Helford River. A wise policy has been the acquiring of coastal property that extends for one farm deep inland, ensuring wider protection of the landscape and good access.

*The charming gatehouse is one of the original parts of Lanhydrock*

## LANHYDROCK  Map ref SW0863

The magnificent Lanhydrock lies about 2½ miles (4km) north of Lostwithiel via the B3268, or can be reached from Bodmin via the A30. It is approached along a splendid avenue of stately beech trees which lead through the beautifully wooded parkland and on first sight the house gives every impression of being wholly Tudor. In fact, all that remains of the original house, built between 1630 and 1642 for the wealthy Truro merchant Sir Richard Robartes, is the gatehouse, entrance porch and north wing. The east wing was removed, and the rest fell victim to a terrible fire in 1881, but, unusually for those times, when most owners would have taken the opportunity to impose the current architectural fashion, the house was rebuilt to match the style of the surviving part. The result is the powerful, dignified building that we see today.

The interiors are very grand, notably the Long Gallery, which has a moulded ceiling showing Old Testament scenes. Throughout the house, the furnishings are lavish and have a comfortable patina of old age. Visitors are, of course, impressed by all this, but they tend to find the greatest fascination within the 'below stairs' sections, including a mighty kitchen, larders, dairy, bakehouse, cellars and servants' quarters.

Lanhydrock is surrounded by beautiful grounds with some pleasant rides and paths to stroll along. Adjoining the house are lovely formal gardens with clipped yews and bronze urns, while the higher garden is famed for its magnolias and rhododendrons.

## LISKEARD   Map ref SX2564

With Bodmin Moor to the north, and Looe to the south, Liskeard is an ideal holiday centre. The town was always of strategic importance, its name translates from 'castle', though no trace remains of any such building. Liskeard was a Coinage town (see page 26) from medieval times and Coinage endowed the town with a status and prosperity which encouraged other business; copper mining during the 19th century further increased the town's prosperity. When mining declined Liskeard continued to thrive as the focus of road and rail communications throughout east Cornwall and is still the northern terminus of the branch railway that connects with Looe.

Today, Liskeard's attractive townscape reflects its prosperous history. The streets, quite narrow in places, are flanked by tall buildings. Fine individual examples include the notable Victorian Webb's Hotel, hip-roofed and stolid, which overlooks the Parade, whilst the Guildhall's Italianate tower dominates Market Street. In Well Lane, off Market Street, is the ancient Pipe Well, an intriguing survival from Liskeard's earliest days; the water is now considered unfit to drink and the well is gated. Liskeard's Church of St Martin, the second largest church in Cornwall after St Petroc's at Bodmin, suffered some heavy-handed Victorian restoration and is rather dull because of it. Liskeard is a busy shopping centre, in keeping with its commercial traditions. On market days, the country comes to town bringing a refreshing bustle to the streets.

### THE LOOE VALLEY LINE

A trip on the Looe Valley Line from Liskeard to Looe is a stress-free and old-fashioned way of going to the seaside and back, recapturing some of the excitement of those days when such a journey as this was a rare treat. The trains descend through steep gradients into the lovely East Looe Valley from Liskeard Station, with station halts on the way giving access to pleasant villages like St Keyne.

*Older slate-hung houses surround Liskeard's handsome Victorian Guildhall in Market Street*

**BIKE TRAILS**

Cycling in the Liskeard and Looe area is well served by the network of quiet lanes that surround the West Looe Valley. Off-road cycling is possible along forestry tracks in Churchbridge and Herodsfoot Woods near the village of Duloe that lies midway between Liskeard and Looe on the B3254. Herodsfoot is about 2 miles (3.2km) north west of Duloe. Please note that cycling is not permitted on public footpaths or on the coast path.

*Fishing boats crowd the harbour at West Looe, a popular centre for shark-fishing*

## LOOE  Map ref SX2553

Looe is in two parts that lie to either side of the merged East and West Looe rivers and they are connected by a road bridge. It was a busy naval town during the 13th and 14th centuries but its long term survival depended on fishing and the import of lime and sand for fertiliser on the farms of the area. A canal linking Looe with Liskeard was built in 1828 and the port prospered on the export of copper from the mines on Bodmin Moor and granite from the moor's Cheesewring Quarry at Minions. The opening of the Liskeard-to-Looe rail link in 1860 was meant to supplement canal trade but the railway overlaid the tow path in so many places that the canal soon declined.

Tourism came early to Looe. It is said that the bathing machine came to Looe beach as early as 1800 when war with France sent the leisured classes to south-west England in search of a home-grown alternative to French resorts. But it was the railway, as always, that led to the growth of the tourism which sustains Looe today.

The old town of East Looe is a delight. There is a European feel in its ordered layout and in the way in which the tall buildings accentuate the narrowness of streets and passageways. The houses, some timber-framed but most of stone, are painted in a variety of colours. The old pilchard-curing cellars by the quay are in unadorned stone and many of the cottages have the characteristic outside stone staircase indicating that the ground floors were used as pilchard processing cellars and net stores. The fishing industry brings a colourful

bustle to the harbour and quayside at East Looe and there is a real sense of sea and town merging. Looe's Banjo Pier can be reached from the quay and the very popular Looe Bay beach adjoins it.

West Looe was always the smaller settlement. It has a lovely outlook across the harbour to East Looe and the older parts of the town around Fore Street and Princes Square have some pleasant features. The way south leads to Marine Drive, from where there are views seaward and to Looe Island. There is a museum in the handsome Old Guildhall in Higher Market Street and a fisheries museum with an aquarium on Buller Quay. Looe has a big car park on the west side of the river at Millpool where there is an excellent Discovery Centre.

The delightful Kilminorth Woods are reached easily from the Millpool car park. Waymarked walks lead through a splendid oak wood and alongside the West Looe River. The woods are rich in plant and insect life and a variety of fascinating wild birds inhabit woods and river. These include herons, which nest in the trees on the opposite bank. Further information can be obtained at the Discovery Centre.

**STARRY-GAZEY PIE**

Starry-gazey pie means what it says – the heads of fish gazing skywards from the crisp golden crust of a pie. Traditionally, the rest of the cleaned fish were baked whole within the pie, amidst slices of hard-boiled eggs and chopped leeks. There are numerous variations, and starry-gazey pie has become the centrepiece of a famous event at Mousehole, near Penzance, on 23 December. This is 'Tom Bowcock's Eve' and commemorates a legendary event in the distant past when local fisherman Tom Bowcock was said to have saved the village from famine by going to sea in a lull in almost continuous stormy weather. Tom – and his cat – returned laden with seven sorts of fish that were soon gazing skywards from scores of pies. Tom and his cat have gained ever more fame as starry characters in a children's book and an animated film.

*A narrow back-street offers a quaint mixture of old buildings, East Looe*

# The Smugglers' Lair

*A delightful, though quite steep and strenuous, walk along the coast west of Looe taking in Talland Bay and the lovely Talland Church. The coast path is rocky in places and can be muddy.*

Time: 2½ hours. Distance: 4 miles (6.4km).
Location: 1¼ miles (2km) south-west of Looe.
Start: National Trust car park near Hendersick Farm, ½ mile (0.8km) off B3359 south-west of Looe.
(OS grid ref: SX236521).
OS Maps: Explorer 107 (St Austell & Liskeard) 1:25,000
Landranger 201 (Plymouth and Launceston) 1:50,000.
See Key to Walks on page 121.

*Treacherous fingers of rock stretch into Talland Bay*

## ROUTE DIRECTIONS

From the entrance to the car park, turn left down the lane into **Talland**, passing Talland Church, then a small car park on your left and the sign for the Smuggler's Rest. Continue along a surfaced lane, then turn left at a junction, signed 'Footpath to Polperro'. Beyond the toilets turn right to walk above **Talland Bay** beach.

At a T-junction, turn left on to a steep surfaced track. Part way up turn left up steps, following coast path sign, to join a rough lane. Bear left on to the coast path at the the entrance to Westfield Old Court. In 250 yards (228m) proceed with care along a rocky section (can be slippery when wet). Pass a war memorial cross on **Downend**

**Point,** climb steeply over bare rock in places, passing a welcome bench. The path soon levels out, then at a junction of paths, turn right and leave the coast path. Head steeply uphill and turn left up steps and alongside the wall of a house. Follow a fenced-in path to a stile, turn left onto a gravelled drive and proceed to a stile and lane.

Turn right, descend very steeply and keep ahead where the lane curves right. From here retrace your earlier steps around Talland Bay beach, back to the Smugglers Rest sign.

By the sign, head diagonally right across a small car park, to a gate and join the coast path. Climb some steep steps, then follow the coast path for half a mile (0.8km) to a stile by a National Trust sign for Hendersick. Keep to the main path and continue to Hore Point. Cross a stile, pass some fangs of rock, then climb steep steps to a welcome seat. There are good views of the off-shore rock called the **Hore Stone**, and of Looe Island.

Continue for a third of a mile (0.5km) to Portnadler Bay, cross a stile and then a second stile. In 30 yards (27m) veer inland (no path), and climb steeply uphill to reach a fence corner. Continue with the fence on your right to a stile, pass a barn, very muddy here, then go through a gate and bear right. In a few yards go left through a small gate. Follow a grassy path to another gate. Cross a farm track, go up through trees to the car park.

### POINTS OF INTEREST

**Talland**
The name Talland may derive from St Tallanus, the adopted name of Talland Church, although the 'lan' component indicates the Cornish term for a sacred place and may reflect the church's ancient provenance. Parts of the present building are believed to date from the 13th century, others from the 15th or 16th centuries. There are some fine features, including the detached tower, and finely carved bench-ends.

**Talland Bay**
The remoteness of Talland Bay made it a smuggling base throughout the 18th and early 19th centuries. An 18th-century vicar and noted exorcist, Richard Dodge, was believed to be closely involved with smuggling and is said to have fostered tales of ghoulish hauntings in the area in order to discourage the curious.

**Downend Point**
The lovely stretch of coast to the east of Downend Point was bequeathed to the National Trust by the author of school stories for girls, Angela Brazil. An early conservationist, she bought the 38 acres in 1922 because she feared that it might be sold for building.

**Hore Stone**
The Hore Stone is more impressive than the modest little headland of Hore Point, close to which it lies. The Hore Stone is crowned with a yellow marine lichen like a dusting of saffron.

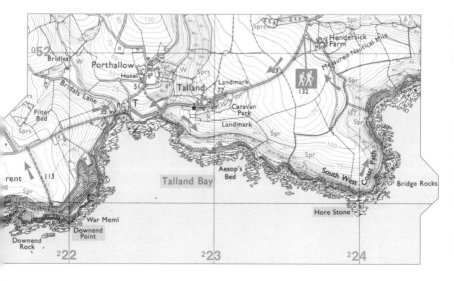

## COINAGE TOWNS

During the 13th century, tin mining in Cornwall became regulated by 'Stannary' districts, centred on the mining areas. Each Stannary (the word derives from the Latin for tin) had its own court and under Stannary law a tinner was exempt from the jurisdiction of all other courts. There was also a Stannary 'Parliament', a tinners' convocation which protected their ancient customs and made their laws. There were also Stannary or 'Coinage' towns where tin was tested for purity by cutting off a small corner, or 'coin', of each block. Once approved the block of tin was stamped with the royal seal of approval, for which a duty was paid to the Crown. The Stannary system is now defunct although some still believe its laws overrule current laws. The original coinage towns were Bodmin, Lostwithiel, Liskeard, Truro and Helston, and later Penzance.

## LOSTWITHIEL  Map ref SX1059

The attractive little town of Lostwithiel was a busy port throughout the medieval period until the silting of the river stopped vessels reaching its quays. Today the river is spanned by a 15th-century bridge with five pointed arches. Like Liskeard, Lostwithiel was a Coinage town, prospering greatly from the revenue from the lucrative administration of tin assaying and approval by royal seal. Near by are the substantial ruins of Restormel Castle (English Heritage), the best preserved military building in Cornwall. The castle was built during the Norman period on the site of a wooden fortification.

Modern Lostwithiel has lost much of its old townscape; the arches and buttresses of the Duchy Palace on Quay Street are all that are left of a much grander complex of buildings that included the Coinage Hall. One special glory is the 13th-century tower and 14th-century spire of the Church of St Bartholomew; the dramatic transition from square to octagon has a pleasing effect. There is a town museum in Fore Street. Coulson Park is by the River Fowey and there are pleasant riverside walks.

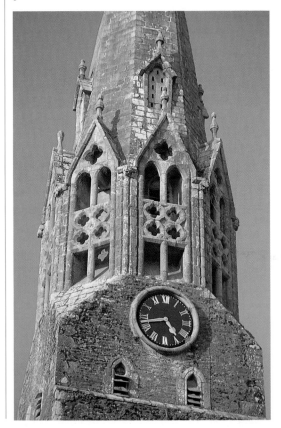

*St Bartholomew's was a Civil War target. Cromwell's army christened a horse 'King Charles' in the church*

## POLPERRO  Map ref SX2051

Polperro rambles delightfully down to the sea. The pattern of narrow lanes and alleyways and steep flanking streets is set by the enclosing walls of the wooded valley within which Polperro lies and is more engaging than in any other Cornish village. The inner harbour sits squarely amidst houses and the boisterous stream, known as the Rafiel, pours into it beneath a Saxon bridge and beside the delightful House On The Props with its rough wooden supports. When the sun shines, Polperro flickers with light and shade. Polperro was always a fishing village, and remains so today though its charm has made it one of the most visited places in Cornwall. Access to Polperro is on foot from a car park at Crumplehorn above the main village. There are shops, art and craft galleries, good pubs and restaurants.

## RAME HEAD  Map ref SX4147

Rame Head is the dramatic western promontory of the Rame Peninsula, with a well preserved example of a typical Iron-Age fort. A medieval chapel and a hermitage once stood here and a small building survives, its roof mottled with moss and lichen, its walls rough with age. A warning beacon was once maintained on Rame Head as an aid to navigation, but tradition speaks of its more likely use by smugglers.

From Rame Head, the great crescent of Whitsand Bay curves to the west. The beach is accessible only at low tide and ways down by steep steps and pathways are limited. Above Whitsand Bay, in a crook of the coast road, is Tregantle Fort, the most westerly of the line of defences that march from Fort Bovisand on the Devon shore of Plymouth Sound through a series of surviving bulwarks. They were built by Lord Palmerston in the 1860s when instability led to the fear of French invasion.

### CORNISH NAMES TO CONJURE WITH

At the western end of Whitsand Bay is the charming little fishing village of Portwrinkle, aptly named for its position on this tucked-in coastline. On the high ground above is the village of Crafthole where there is a fine old pub called the Finnygook, a name to conjure with on dark windy nights. It is thought to relate to part of the neighbouring coastline, although its meaning is obscure. There are even odder local names, of course, such as Portugal Pump and Eglarooze Cliff.

*Looking westward to Rame Head from Penlee Point*

# South-east Cornwall: Looe, Liskeard and Fowey

Leisure Information

Places of Interest

Shopping

The Performing Arts

Sports, Activities and the Outdoors

Annual Events and Customs

**Checklist** ✓

## Leisure Information

### TOURIST INFORMATION CENTRES

**Fowey**
The Ticket Shop, Post Office, 4 Custom House Hill. Tel: 01726 833616.
**Looe**
The Guildhall, Fore St, East Looe. Tel: 01503 262072 (Open Easter–Oct).
**Lostwithiel**
Community Centre, Liddicoat Road. Tel: 01208 872207.

### OTHER INFORMATION

**Coastguard**
Dial 999 and ask for the Coastguard Service, which co-ordinates lifeboats and cliff rescue.
**Cornwall Wildlife Trust**
Five Acres, Allet, Truro. Tel: 01872 73939.
**English Heritage**
Portland House, Stag Place London. Tel: 0171 973 3434.
**Health**
Information on health problems is available Tel: 0800 665544. Dental Helpline Tel: 0800 371192.
**Environment Agency**
Manley House, Kestrel Way, Exeter. Tel: 01392 444000.

**National Trust in Cornwall**
Cornwall Regional Office, Lanhydrock, Bodmin. Tel: 01208 74281.
**Parking**
Weekly ticket covers use of car parks at Looe (Millpool) and at Cawsand. Day Rover ticket covers use of car parks at Cawsand, Portwrinkle, Seaton and Looe (Millpool). Tickets are available from the pay-and-display machines at the car parks.
**Public Transport**
Timetable covering all bus, coach, rail, ferry and air services in Cornwall is available from Passenger Transport Unit, County Hall, Truro. Tel: 01872 322000.
**South West Water**
Highercombe Park, Lewdown, Okehampton. For enquiries on recreation/fishing Tel: 01837 871565.
**Surf Call**
Report on local surfing conditions. Tel: 0891 333080.
**Weather Call**
South-west weather details. Tel: 0891 500758.

### ORDNANCE SURVEY MAPS

Explorer 1:25,000 Sheets 107, 108, 109.
Landranger 1:50,000 Sheets 190, 200, 201.

## Places of Interest

There will be an admission charge at the following places of interest unless otherwise stated.
**Antony House**
Torpoint. Tel: 01752 812191. Open: Apr–Oct, certain days.
**Carnglaze Slate Caverns**
St Neot. Tel: 01579 320251. Open: Easter–Sep, daily.
**Colliford Lake**
near Bolventor, Bodmin Moor. Tel: 01579 342366.
**Cotehele**
St Dominick, near Calstock. Tel: 01579 350434. Open: house Apr–Oct, except Fri; garden all year.
**Fowey Aquarium**
Town Quay. Open: Easter–Oct.
**Fowey Museum**
Town Hall, Trafalgar Square. Open: Easter week, then Spring Bank Hol–Sep, Christmas; weekdays.
**Jamaica Inn and Museums**
Bolventor. Tel: 01566 86250. Daphne du Maurier room, Mr Potter's Museum of Curiosities (Victorian taxidermy). Open: daily; Museum daily, except Christmas.
**Lanhydrock**
near Bodmin. Tel: 01208 73320. Open: Apr–Oct, house most days; garden daily.

**Lanreath Farm and Folk Museum**
Lanreath, near Lostwithiel. Tel: 01503 220321. Open: Easter–Oct, daily.

**Liskeard Museum**
West Street. Tel: 01579 345407. Open: May–Sep, daily.

**Living From the Sea**
Buller Quay Fish Market, East Looe. Tel: 01752 344383. Museum of fishing and local sea life aquarium. Open: Easter–Oct, daily.

**Looe Valley Line**
Liskeard–Looe, with request stops on the way. Tel: 0345 484950.

**Lostwithiel Museum**
Fore Street. Open: Easter and Bank Hol Mon May–Sep, most days. Free.

**Lynher Valley Dairy**
Upton Cross, near Liskeard. Tel: 01579 362244. Home of Yarg cheese, guided tours. Open: Easter–Oct, most days.

**The Monkey Sanctuary**
St Martins, Looe. Tel: 01503 262532. Open: 2 weeks at Easter and May–Sep, most days.

**Mount Edgcumbe House**
Cremyll. Tel: 01752 822236. Open: house and Earls Garden, Apr–Oct; visitor centre Apr–Oct, daily; park and formal gardens, all year, daily.

**Old Guildhall Museum**
Higher Market Street, East Looe. Tel: 01503 263709. Open: Easter week, then May–Sep, most days.

**Restormel Castle**
near Lostwithiel. Tel: 01208 872687. Open: all year, daily.

**St Catherine's Castle**
Readymoney Cove. Free.

**St Winnow Barton Farm Museum**
St Winnow, Lostwithiel. Tel: 01208 873742. Open: Easter–Oct, daily. Free.

**South-east Cornwall Discovery Centre**
Millpool, West Looe. Tel: 01503 262777. Open: Mar–Sep, most days.

**Tamar Valley Line**
Gunnislake–Plymouth, via Calstock. Tel: 0345 484950. Various special trips including combined boat and rail trips.

SPECIAL INTEREST FOR CHILDREN

The following places may be of interest to visitors with children. Unless otherwise stated there will be an admission charge.

**Dobwalls Family Adventure Park**
Dobwalls, near Liskeard. Tel: 01579 320325/321129. Miniature western railways; 8 adventure play areas; art gallery. Open: Apr–Sep, daily; Oct weekends and half-term.

**Land of Legend and Model Village**
Polperro. Tel: 01503 272378. Polperro in miniature; model railway. Open: Easter–Oct, daily.

**Paul Corin's Magnificent Music Machines**
St Keyne Station, between Liskeard and Looe. Tel: 01579 343108. Fairground and Wurlitzer organs. Open: Easter–end Oct, daily.

**Porfell Animal Land**
Lanreath, near Lostwithiel. Tel: 01503 220211. Small farm with domestic, wild and exotic animals; woodland walks. Open: Easter–Oct, daily.

**Tamar Valley Donkey Park**
St Ann's Chapel, Gunnislake. Tel: 01822 834072. Attractions include donkey rides, woodland walks. Open: Apr–Oct daily; Nov–Mar weekends.

## Shopping

**Fowey**
Antique shops, galleries and craft shops in the Fore Street area.

**Liskeard**
Open-air market with farm produce a speciality, Dean Street Cattle Market, Mon and Thu. Trago Mills Shopping Centre, Two Waters Foot. Large shopping complex on the A38, about 4 miles (6.4km) west of Liskeard.

**Lostwithiel**
Good selection of antique shops in Fore Street.

LOCAL SPECIALITIES

**Craft workshops**
Lanreath Farm and Folk Museum, Lanreath, near Lostwithiel. Open: daily Easter–Oct. Tel: 01503 220321.

**Pottery**
Fowey Pottery, 10a Passage Street, Fowey. Tel: 01726 833099. Millstream Pottery, Fowey. Tel: 01726 832512. Louis Hudson Pottery Limited, Unit 8, Moorswater Industrial Estate, Liskeard. Tel: 01579 342864. The Pottery Shop, Quay Road, Polperro. Tel: 01503 272307.

**Woollens**
Kernow Mill, Trerulefoot, Saltash. Tel: 01752 851898. Open all year except Christmas and Easter Sun.

## The Performing Arts

**Sterts Arts and Environmental Centre**
Upton Cross, near Liskeard. Tel: 01579 362382/362962. Drama, music, dance, arts and environmental exhibition gallery. Centre open all year; theatre season Jun–Sep.

## Sports, Activities and the Outdoors

ANGLING

**Sea**
There are day and half-day trips from Fowey, Looe and Polruan. Shark-fishing from Looe. *Looe*: Looe Chandlery Tel: 01503 264355; The Tackle Shop Tel: 01503 262189.

*Looe is the centre of Britain's shark fishing*

## Fly

East and West Looe rivers (salmon, sea trout and brown trout). All year. Permits from Looe Post Office Tel: 01503 262110; Siblyback Water Park (rainbow trout); Colliford Lake (brown trout). Permits on site. Ranger Tel: 01579 342366.

### BEACHES

**Kingsand and Cawsand**
Small safe beaches. Dogs not allowed at Cawsand Beach.
**Looe**
Hannafore Beach: long stretches of shingle and some sand; East Looe and Plaidy Beach: popular, busy beach. Dogs not allowed; Millendreath Beach, near Looe: Small family beach close to Millendreath Holiday Park where many facilities are open to day visitors; Seaton Beach: large sand and pebble beach.
**Whitsand Bay**
3-mile (4.8km) stretch of sandy beach but with limited and steep access. Rip currents can make bathing unsafe at times. Lifeguards patrol from mid-June to mid-Sep.
There are small beaches at Readymoney Cove, Fowey (very busy), Lantivet Bay and Talland Bay near Polperro.
Dogs are not allowed on several popular beaches from Easter to October. During winter, when dogs are allowed, owners must use poop scoops.
Many beaches have Water Safety Information Points.

### BOAT TRIPS

**Fowey**
River cruises, motor boat hire. Foy–Lostwithiel can be booked through Fowey Tourist Information Centre, for other trips, see information boards at harbour.
**Looe**
Sea cruises available. See information boards at the harbour.
**Saltash**
Tamar Expeditions, Tinnel, Landulph, Saltash. Tel: 01579 351113. Accompanied kayak expeditions. Booking essential.

### BOWLING

The bowling clubs at Fowey and Lostwithiel welcome visitors. For further information contact the local Tourist Information Centre.

### COUNTRY PARKS & WOODS

**Cardinham Woods**
near Bodmin. Tel: 01392 832262. Waymarked walks, cycle trail, cycle hire, café.
**Kilminorth Woods**
Alongside West Looe River. Waymarked walks. Information from Discovery Centre, Millpool car park. Tel: 01503 262777.
**Mount Edgcumbe Country Park**
Cremyll. Tel: 01752 822236. Open: all year, daily.

### CYCLING

A network of quiet lanes offers good cycling between the main roads and main centres of the area. The following woodland areas have excellent cycle routes; leaflets are available from Looe Discovery Centre. Tel: 01503 262777.

Cardinham Woods, near Bodmin. Tel: 01392 832262. Duloe, Churchbridge and Herodsfoot Woods. Kilminorth Woods, Looe.

Cycling is not allowed on public footpaths or on the coast path.

### CYCLE HIRE

**Bodmin**
Glynn Valley Cycle Hire, Cardinham Woods, Margate. Tel: 01208 74244.
**Liskeard**
Liskeard Cycle Centre, Pig Meadow Lane. Tel: 01579 347696.
**Looe**
Looe Mountain Bike Hire. Tel: 01503 262877/263871.

### GOLF COURSES

**Lanhydrock**
Lanhydrock Golf Club, Lostwithiel Rd. Tel: 01208 73600.
**Looe**
Looe Golf Club, Bin Down. Tel: 01503 240239.

**Lostwithiel**
Lostwithiel Golf and Country Club, Lower Polscoe. Tel: 01208 873550.
**Portwrinkle**
Whitsand Bay Hotel, Golf and Country Club. Tel: 01503 230470.
**St Mellion**
St Mellion Golf and Country Club, near Saltash. Tel: 01579 351351.
**Saltash**
China Fleet Golf and Country Club. Tel: 01752 848668.

### HORSE-RIDING

**Liskeard**
TM International School of Horsemanship, Sunrise Riding Centre, Henwood. Tel: 01579 362895.

### SAILING

The Royal Fowey Yacht Club. Tel: 01726 832245/833573. Fowey Gallants. Tel: 01726 832335.
Looe Sailing Club, Buller Street, Looe. Tel: 01503 262559.

### WATERSPORTS

**Liskeard**
Siblyback Watersports Centre, Common Moor. Tel: 01579 346522. Windsurfing, sailing, kayaking. Equipment hire, qualified instruction. Open: Apr–Oct daily.
**Saltash**
See under Boat Trips.

## Annual Events and Customs

**Fowey**
Fowey Regatta. Major regatta held in August.

The checklists give details of just some of the facilities within this guide. Further information can be obtained from Tourist Information Centres.

# North Cornwall: Bodmin, Bude, Launceston and Padstow

North Cornwall has spectacular stretches of coastline where a ten minute walk can lead to the solitude of quiet coves and wooded valleys. Yet the region has easily accessible beaches where even on the busiest days there is room to spare. Padstow, Tintagel and Boscastle each have uniquely contrasting appeal and, away from the coast, tree-dappled lanes link charming villages. On the ancient landscape of the high moorland, wind-sculpted granite rocks lie scattered across the lonely hills of Rough Tor and Brown Willy and, at Launceston and Bodmin, the spirit of Old Cornwall still lingers amidst the weathered stonework.

## BODMIN  Map ref SX0667

The town of Bodmin lies on the south-western fringe of Bodmin Moor. It hardly seems part of the wild country to which it gives its name, although it clings to its own high hill, The Beacon. Bodmin was once the county town of Cornwall, but has long since relinquished that status to Truro.

The town's development began in the 10th century when the monastery founded by St Petroc at Padstow was destroyed by Viking raiders. The monks withdrew inland for safety's sake and established their new foundation at Bodmin. They brought the holy remains of St Petroc with them and turned the town into the most important medieval religious site in Cornwall. Bodmin's name derives from 'menegh' meaning monks, and 'bos' meaning house. Augustinian monks later adopted the monastery, Franciscans founded a priory here, and the Shrine of St Petroc transformed Bodmin into a place of pilgrimage.

The Reformation, and Henry VIII's Dissolution of the Monasteries brought decline, although Bodmin retained strategic importance for a time because of its position on the main route through Cornwall. Today, though Bodmin has lost much of its historic status, its robust Cornish character and strong community spirit remain intact. Bodmin is the ideal centre from which to explore north and south-east Cornwall.

### STEAMING UP

The Bodmin and Wenford Railway operates steam trains along a delightful rural line from Bodmin to Bodmin Parkway Station, which is on the main Paddington to Penzance line. A branch line also goes west to Boscarne from where the Camel Trail (see page 48) can be joined. The restored Great Western Railway station in Bodmin is the headquarters and main station of the line. It is reached, from the centre of Bodmin, along St Nicholas Street, the B3268, and connections with main line services can be made at Bodmin Parkway. Passengers for the Bodmin and Wenford Railway are not allowed to park at the main line station.

*Peaceful today, the town of Bodmin was a hotbed of Cornish rebellion in the 15th and 16th centuries*

**BACK LANES BY BIKE**
To the north of Bodmin, narrow winding lanes link the charming villages of Helland, Helland Bridge, Blisland, St Breward, St Tudy and St Mabyn. This is an area of peaceful mixed countryside and although divided by the B3266, the network of lanes connect across the main road at various points. The area can be reached from the Camel Trail, and offers some delightful cycling and testing navigation. There are steep inclines, but there is always the prospect of a pleasant inn, and an occasional cream tea halt along the way. There are cool, quiet churches too. A good circular tour from Bodmin links Helland Bridge, Blisland, St Breward, St Tudy and St Mabyn.

Bodmin has some outstanding architecture, including a neo-classical court building of 1873 situated in Mount Folly. In Fore Street there are attractive stucco façades and the old cattle market has Doric piers and an entertaining frieze of rams' and bulls' heads. The Church of St Petroc is the largest church in Cornwall and has some fine features. Bodmin Museum is in Mount Folly Square, on the site of the old Franciscan Priory, and The Duke of Cornwall's Light Infantry Museum is housed in the Keep of the Victorian barracks. The Bodmin and Wenford Steam Railway Station is in St Nicholas Street.

## BOSCASTLE   Map ref SX0990

The sea can surge in and out of Boscastle harbour in a menacing way, entering between looming cliffs of slate and shale. The outer walls of the harbour are always damp with the sea and the salt air. Most of the area is owned by the National Trust, as are the adjoining clifflands of Willapark to the south and Penally to the north. The blow-hole in Penally Point, the headland on the northern side of the harbour entrance, is known as the Devil's Bellows and when tide and sea conditions are right, it throws a spectacular spout of spray across the harbour entrance.

Boscastle was a busy commercial port throughout the 19th century – sea transport was usual throughout north Cornwall until the railway arrived in the 1890s. Up to 200 ships called at Boscastle in any one year, carrying coal and limestone from South Wales, wines and spirits, general goods and even timber from Bristol. Cargoes out of Boscastle included china clay and slate, and manganese from a mine in the Valency Valley above the village. Boscastle harbour was always difficult to enter and sailing vessels had to be towed through the entrance by eight-man rowing boats and by horses on tow paths. When big swells threatened to drive vessels against the walls of the channel, hawser ropes were made fast to the vessel from both shores, where teams of men braced the ropes round granite posts to hold the vessel in mid-channel.

Even on land there was no easy exit out of Boscastle and teams of horses hauled loaded carts up and down the steep roads which today carry modern traffic. The valley of the River Valency runs inland from Boscastle through deep woods, a peaceful contrast to the threatening sea.

Boscastle village proper is on the high ground and has some fine old buildings. There is a large car park near the harbour and an excellent visitor centre. On the north side of the harbour a National Trust information centre and shop is housed in an old blacksmith's forge. Among the village pubs are the Wellington near the harbour and the Napoleon at the top end of the main village; Napoleon being on top is a mere quirk of course. In dull weather, Boscastle can have a certain eeriness, which may explain the presence of a Museum of Witchcraft in the Witches House by the harbour.

On Forrabury Common, to the south of Boscastle, the National Trust has preserved the pattern of Iron-Age land tenure, whereby long narrow strips of land were cultivated under a system called 'stitchmeal'. These Forrabury Stitches are still cultivated by tenants.

**TEA AND SYMPATHY**

The coast path leads south from Boscastle Harbour, first by a steep path that leads to the summit of Willapark. The white-washed building on top of Willapark is said to have been built by a local merchant in the early 19th century at a time when 'tea houses', or the more suggestive 'pleasure' houses were fashionable and where the local gentry repaired for tea and sympathy, or stronger spirits, at weekends. It was used subsequently as a lookout.

*Boscastle, with a steep road running down to the harbour, was a favourite haunt of Thomas Hardy*

## ST JULIOT'S CHURCH AND THE POET

The Valency Valley is a romantic place with a romantic story, for it was here that the young Thomas Hardy wooed his wife-to-be, Emma Gifford. In his capacity as an architect, he came to help in the restoration of St Juliot's Church, where he met and fell in love with the vicar's young sister-in-law. Sadly, their marriage proved to be less than idyllic, but after his wife's death Hardy wrote many love poems about their days in the Boscastle area.

*Rocky Valley, north-east of Bossiney, opens out onto the rugged coastline*

## BOSSINEY   Map ref SX0688

Bossiney, a short distance from busy Tintagel, is a quiet relief from too much Arthurian legend. Much of the coast at Bossiney is in the care of the National Trust. The beach below the cliffs at Bossiney Haven is reached by a steep path where donkeys once carried seaweed up from the beach to be used as fertiliser on neighbouring fields.

A short distance to the east lies Rocky Valley, where the river cuts through a final rock barrier into the sea. At the heart of the valley are the ruins of an old woollen mill. Within the ruins are small maze carvings on natural rock, claimed by some to date from the Bronze Age, but more likely to be Victorian. Rocky Valley's river can be followed inland through the wooded St Nectan's Glen to St Nectan's Kieve, where a 60-foot (18m) waterfall plunges down a dark, mist-shrouded ravine. Here, in the 6th century, St Nectan is said to have meditated, rather wetly. The Kieve is pleasantly gloomy and atmospheric. King Arthur enthusiasts, not surprisingly, are thrilled. There is a fee to view the falls and there is a tea-garden above. The site can be reached by following a public footpath which starts behind the Rocky Valley Centre at Trethevy on the B3263 a mile (1.6km) north-east of Bossiney.

## BUDE  Map ref SS2105

There are few more exhilarating beaches than Bude's Summerleaze when the sea rolls onto the sand in long, unbroken waves. But there is more to Bude than beaches. The Bude Canal shaped much of the immediate hinterland of Bude Harbour and is now a popular attraction (see Walk on page 36). The canal was built in the early 19th century to carry calcium-rich sand to inland farms where it was used to enrich the soil. The canal reached nearly to Launceston, but its full potential was never realised and its use declined by the middle of that century. This history of the canal is illustrated in The Bude-Stratton Museum at The Old Forge on the Lower Wharf.

Bude is a busy, friendly town – The Strand and Belle Vue are the main shopping streets. There is a good visitor centre in the car park near the harbour. A series of easily accessible and attractive beaches stretch north from Bude: Crooklets, Northcott Mouth and Sandy Mouth. The last two are almost covered at high tide. There are pleasant walks along the coast path to the north where the cliff-top area is level, cropped grassland. To the south of Bude, via a scenic coast road, is the vast expanse of Widemouth Bay.

Bude has few traditional buildings. The town evolved in the 19th century from a small fishing port through the grafting on of functional buildings, first for commerce, then for tourism. But just inland is Stratton, a medieval market town with a history that pre-dates Anglo-Saxon times. Stratton was the chief settlement of the area until Bude's ascendancy during the 19th century, and has some fine old buildings, a handsome church and traditional pubs of great character.

*Massive stone piers guard the sea-entrance to the old Bude Canal*

### STRATTON STROLL

Stratton was a busy market town for centuries and its attractive, narrow streets reflect its ancient tradition. Just north of Stratton is Stamford Hill, site of a Civil War battle of 1643 where Sir Bevil Grenville, of nearby Stowe, led a Cornish Royalist army to victory. A quiet stroll through Stratton is very rewarding. The town is reached by turning off onto the Holsworthy road from the A39, just east of Bude. There is a car park at Howells Bridge on the eastern edge of Stratton. From the car park, a walk up Spicer's Lane leads to the church and the centre of the town.

# Canal and Cliffs at Bude

*A peaceful walk along the banks of the surviving section of the old Bude Canal. The route then crosses fields to link up with the coast path which leads back to Bude along rolling clifflands and above white breakers. This is easy walking with only a few inclines, but the field section may be muddy.*

Time: 2½ hours. Distance: 5 miles (8km).
Location: Bude, 1 mile (1.6km) off the A39 at Stratton.
Start: Crescent car park near the town centre.
(OS grid ref: SS208062).
OS Maps: Explorer 111 (Bude, Boscastle &Tintagel) 1:25,000
Landranger 190 (Bude and Clovelly) 1:50,000.
See Key to Walks on page 121.

## ROUTE DIRECTIONS

Follow the surfaced track that leads inland along the east bank of the **Bude Canal** and pass a bird hide on the left overlooking Bude Marshes Nature Reserve. Continue alongside the canal, changing to the west bank at Rodd's Bridge. Pass two locks, then a large weir at Whalesborough, where the canal leads off from the River Neet. Soon reach a wooden footbridge that leads

*Lock gates overlook the sandy beach at Bude*

across the canal to the busy A39 and **Helebridge** (cross the bridge and the A39 to visit Helebridge). Keeping to the main route do not cross bridge, but go over stile, signed 'Widemouth Bay'. Follow canal bank to another stile on to a surfaced farm track, then where the track bends right, climb a waymarked stile by a gate on the left and follow a field track uphill over the brow of the field to reach a stile by a gate. Maintain course uphill to a further stile, then keep to the left-hand hedge of the next field to reach a stile. Bear slightly left across the next field, cross a stile, then follow the right-hand edge of the field for a short distance before veering diagonally left to the bottom of the field to reach a stile and the coast road.

Cross the road, then take the right-hand track towards the sea to join the coast path, to the right of the old **Salthouse**. Turn right, taking care where the path passes close to the cliff edge, and follow the acorn waymarkers round Lower Longbeak Point.

At Upton follow the path along a fenced-in section, then go through a gate onto open grassland. Continue past a coastguard exercise pole and climb steadily to the summit of **Efford Beacon** where there is a very welcome seat and a good viewpoint.

Proceed along the coast path, descending to **Compass Point** and its old watchtower. Turn right and cross a grassy area to reach a stile on to a rough track. Turn right along the track, and then along a surfaced road, passing a church. Cross the canal bridge and return to the car park.

## POINTS OF INTEREST

**Bude Canal**
The canal was opened during the 1820s and linked Bude to Druxton Wharf, just north of Launceston. The main cargo was sea sand which farmers spread on their calcium-deficient fields. Coal, timber and farm goods were also transported inland, with grain and other produce carried on the return journey. The canal became uneconomical by the 1860s and was officially closed in 1891.

**Helebridge**
Materials were shipped along the Bude Canal in tub boats. Helebridge was a staging post where the boats were hoisted up the Marhamchurch incline plane to be re-floated at the next level. The tub boats had iron wheels and they were hauled up incline planes on chains attached to counterweights. The counterweights were large iron buckets that were filled with water and then lowered

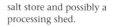

down a deep shaft at the top of the incline. There is a small museum of canal exhibits and the surviving Marhamchurch incline is easily reached from the museum.

**The Salthouse**
Seine netting for pilchards and mullet was probably carried out in Widemouth Bay. This much-changed building, now a private house, at the cliff edge was a salt store and possibly a processing shed.

**Efford Beacon**
The cliffs along this stretch of coastline are composed of interspersed bands of sandstone and shale that were folded and twisted by massive earth-building movements some 200 million years ago.

**Compass Point**
The old watchtower on this headland is known as the Temple of the Winds. It was built in the 1820s as an early form of coastguard station, controlling shipping movements in and out of Bude. It was dismantled once and re-erected further inland because of cliff-erosion, a continuing threat.

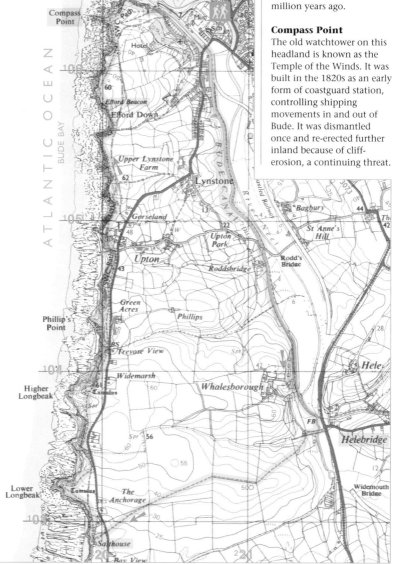

*Crackington Haven is a good starting point for coastal walks*

**CRACKINGTON COAST WALKS**

The stretch of coast around Crackington Haven can be reached less strenuously from the sturdy little Church of St Genny's, just north of Crackington Haven. The coast road south of Crackington is well-supplied with parking spaces that give access to National Trust cliff land above Strangles Beach. This whole area of cliff has been altered by landslips, and though the coast path is safe and stable, walkers should not stray from it. Just off the coast road is the National Trust farm at Trevigue where refreshments are available during the season. Below the farm is a wooded valley through which a fine walk leads down into Crackington Haven.

**CRACKINGTON HAVEN**  Map ref SX1496

The mighty bulwark of cliff at Crackington is best viewed from the southern approach. It seems to dwarf the cove and beach, its twisted and folded shale mellowed by swathes of grass and sedge. Crackington was a haven of sorts during the 19th century, but it was a port in the most basic sense – small vessels simply ran onto the sand as the tide dropped, to offload limestone and coal and to load slates.

The beach at Crackington is rather scant and stony, but the surroundings are pleasant and coastal walks to either side are magnificent. The coast path from Crackington Haven leads north to Castle Point. Take a deep breath for the climb out of the cove. There are the remnants of Iron-Age embankments at Castle Point. A mile or so further on is Dizzard Point where an old oak wood clings to the slopes.

**DELABOLE**  Map ref SX0683

Slate is believed to have been quarried at Delabole as early as medieval times. At 500 feet (152m) this is the deepest quarry in England; it is still being worked and its remarkable proportions can be seen from a public viewing platform. There is a showroom near by. Delabole is a quarrying village with the sturdy character of similar communities in north Wales.

About a mile (1.6km) north of Delabole, along the B3314, is the first commercial wind farm to be established in Britain. The ten great white towers and their whirling vanes are quite sculptural, generating

electricity for 3,000 homes. They can be easily seen from a viewing area, and the adjoining visitor centre outlines the history of wind farms with displays, models and educational material. Just south of Delabole is St Teath, a pretty village with an attractive church that has a refreshingly spacious interior.

## LAUNCESTON  Map ref SX3384

If Cornwall needs a metaphorical 'gateway', then Launceston qualifies, castle and all, but take care how you pronounce Launceston: say 'Lanson' – or else. Launceston was once a walled town, known as Dunheved, a powerful Norman stronghold, and the capital of Cornwall.

The legacy of the town's long history is its good architecture and the rather convoluted plan of its streets. To enjoy Launceston, park as soon as you can (there are car parks near the market and at Thomas Road and Tower Street) – Launceston's handsome South Gate forces traffic to pass through in single-file while pedestrians pass comfortably three abreast beneath an adjacent arch.

At the centre of the town is the Square. There are some very fine Georgian buildings, including the White Hart Hotel, which has the added flourish of a Norman arch over its doorway. The entrance to Launceston Castle (English Heritage) is reached by going down Western Road from the Square. It is impressive still, and though much has been lost, the typical motte-and-bailey structure survives. The stone keep and ruined gatehouse of the motte dominate the highest point of the complex. The clay and rubble walls of the castle seem fragile enough now, but the overall impression is still one of strength and dominance.

*Delabole boasts the biggest man-made hole in the country, in its ancient slate quarry*

### OTTER SANCTUARY

The Tamar Otter Sanctuary is at North Petherwin, which is reached by turning west off the B3254 at Langdon Cross, about 3 miles (4.8km) north of Launceston. Here the Otter Trust rehabilitates and breeds otters for introduction to the wild. Dormice and several species of deer feature amongst other attractions.

## JOHN WESLEY AND METHODISM

During the 18th century the uncertainties of mining and fishing resulted in periodic unemployment and hunger. The established Church was seen as the preserve of the gentry. Amidst these negative forces, the natural spirit of the Cornish people survived, but without direction. Violence drunkenness, neglect and even riot were commonplace. Into this spiritual vacuum came the charismatic John and Charles Wesley to preach redemption and passionate non-conformity. Charles Wesley came first, but it was John who made Cornwall his special preserve, visiting about 40 times in 39 years.

*The ornate carving on the outside walls of St Mary Magdalene's church commemorates the wife of Sir Henry Trecarrel*

In contrast to friable clay, Launceston's Church of St Mary Magdalene displays granite at its ornamental extreme. Every inch of this 16th-century building is covered with intricate carving. Pevsner called it 'barbarous profuseness'. Stand back, and admire. The Launceston Steam Railway is based at the bottom end of St Thomas Road and runs for a delightful 2 miles (3.2km) through the valley of the Kensey River. There is an engineering exhibition at the station.

The village of Altarnun lies on the edge of Bodmin Moor about 7 miles (11.2km) west of Launceston. There is a car park just off the A30, from where it is a short walk to the village. The Church of St Nonna, known as the 'Cathedral of the Moor', has a noble tower and a spacious interior with some elegant features. These include a beautifully decorated Norman font and a large number of bench-ends with fine carvings. Cottages and other buildings in Altarnun are very fine. Neville Northey Burnard, the 19th-century sculptor, was born here, and his work can be seen in an early sculpture of the head of John Wesley, displayed above the door of the old Methodist chapel. He was also responsible for the Lander Memorial at the top of Truro's Lemon Street.

A fine contrast to Altarnun's 'Cathedral' is the Wesleyan Isbell Cottage at nearby Trewint. Here John Wesley and his fellow preachers stayed during their many visits to Cornwall in the 18th century. Digory Isbell, whose house it was, added a special 'prophet's chamber', now restored and still very tranquil.

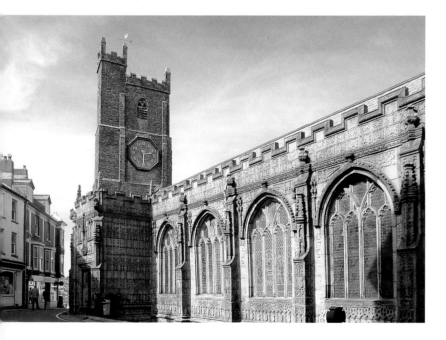

*Rolling surf at Duckpool*

**MORWENSTOW AND COOMBE**  Map ref SS2015
The parish of Morwenstow lies at the northern extreme
of Cornwall in the narrow corridor of land that the
infant Tamar withholds from Devon. Its coast is
awesome, yet unexpected when approached across the
flat green fields that end without much warning at the
edge of 300-foot (91.5m) cliffs. This is the land of the
famous Culm Measures, great twisted slabs of layered
shale that rise from remote boulder beaches that are
ribbed with fins of sea-washed rock.

Its natural beauty apart, Morwenstow owes much to
the reputation of the Victorian parson, eccentric, and
poet manqué, Robert Stephen Hawker, who was vicar at
the Church of St Morwenna for many years. The church
has good Norman features and is beautifully situated
amidst trees in a shallow combe that leads towards the
sea. The interior of the church has great repose and is
pleasantly melancholy, especially at dusk, when there is
a wonderful feeling of isolation. Visit Morwenstow with
time to spare. The land surrounding the church, and the
stretch of cliffs to the west, are owned and conserved by
the National Trust.

South from Morwenstow is Coombe hamlet, in a
wooded valley that continues the theme of tranquillity.
The river reaches the sea at Duckpool where the pebble
beach has built up to dam a small pool of fresh water.
Just north of Coombe, the coast path passes above Lower
Sharpnose Point, where spectacular natural piers of rock
jut out into the sea like the massive walls of ruined
temples. Inland the smooth dishes of the Cleave Camp
Satellite Station strike an incongruous note amidst such
raw beauty.

**THE HAWKER ENIGMA**
Morwenstow's Victorian vicar,
Robert Stephen Hawker, was a
marvellous eccentric, devoted
to recovering the bodies of
drowned sailors who were in
no short supply along this
treacherous coast. But
Hawker's stay at Morwenstow
was fruitful in other ways. He
is credited with reintroducing
Harvest Festival celebrations,
and he wrote the famous *Song
of the Western Men*, now
Cornwall's anthem, especially
at rugby matches. Hawker
built a new vicarage – three of
its chimneys were modelled
on the towers of favourite
churches; another on the
tower of an Oxford college.
The kitchen chimney was a
model of his mother's tomb.
While the chimneys smoked,
Hawker is said to have smoked
opium. He also dressed up as
a mermaid on occasions. Say
no more!

# Caverns and Quiet Coves

*An exhilarating walk round Stepper Point and along the shores of the Camel Estuary overlooking the notorious Doom Bar, returning via field paths inland and a final stroll past some spectacular coastal features. Quite strenuous in places but generally flat walking. Great care needed near the cliff edge.*

Time: 3 hours. Distance: 5 miles (8km).
Location: 1½ miles (2.4km) north of Padstow.
Start: Small parking area just north of Crugmeer, 1½ miles (2.4km) off the B3276 near Padstow. (OS grid ref: SW900771).
OS Maps: Explorer 106 (Newquay & Padstow) 1:25,000
Landranger 200 (Newquay and Bodmin) 1:50,000.
See Key to Walks on page 121.

## ROUTE DIRECTIONS

From the parking area above the bend in the road, cross the road diagonally right to join a permissive path beyond a stile. On reaching the coast path, turn right across a stone stile, following the path above

*Hawker's Cove was formerly the site of a busy coastguard and lifeboat station*

the spectacular Butter Hole.

Bear left at an acorn signpost along the cliff edge, pass through a gap in an old wall, then turn right onto a grassy track to pass Pepper Hole away to your left. It is a vast gulf in the cliff and should only be approached with great caution.

Continue along the coast path to pass the Pepperpot tower on **Stepper Point**. Cross over a track then in half a mile (0.8km) reach **Hawker's Cove**. Follow signs to the road on the other side of the cove. Turn left, then on the bend, bear off left with coast path to pass behind the old lifeboat station and proceed to Harbour Cove.

Follow the path along the side of the Cove to where steps lead down left to a sandy track. Cross the track, go over a wooden footbridge and pass through trees to reach a field. Keep to the left-hand edge for about 100 yards (91m), then bear off left by iron railings, to reach a sandy track. Turn right and keep ahead up a broad stony farm track to Tregirls Farm, and join a surfaced lane.

Shortly cross a stile on your right, then head diagonally right across a field to a stile and maintain direction across a further six fields via connecting stiles, to reach a lane and the hamlet of Crugmeer. Turn left, pass between cottages, then at a T-junction turn right for a few yards, before bearing left down a surfaced lane that leads in three quarters of a mile (1.2km) to the edge of Trevone.

Here, follow the coast path right up some steps. Soon, go left over a stile and continue along the unprotected cliff edge, then steeply uphill, with the astonishing chasm of **Round Hole** to your right, the rim of which should be approached with great care.

Continue along the coast path to pass above the ridge-like **Porthmissen Bridge** and the Marble Cliffs, then the huge gulf of Longcarrow Cove and on towards the offshore stacks of The Meropes. Pass through an area of gullies and small streams, follow a winding path into a dip, cross a final stream, then bear right away from the coast path and follow a permissive path inland to reach a stile and the road by the parking area.

### POINTS OF INTEREST

**Doom Bar**
The Camel Estuary is deep with sand, and the notorious Doom Bar lies just below the surface, its shifting sands making navigation difficult and, in rough weather, very dangerous.

**Stepper Point**
The resistant greenstone rock of Stepper Point was once quarried for roadstone. On the summit of the Point stands the Pepperpot tower. Such structures were a common feature of estuaries and river mouths. They were used by sailors as daymarks by which to calculate their often tortuous ways into port.

**Hawker's Cove**
The grimly unstylish buildings above the cove were originally coastguard houses, with the attractive lower row of dwellings once housing estuary pilots. A lifeboat house was built at the head of the cove in 1827. It was replaced by the larger building that still stands beside the coast path, though it ceased to be a lifeboat house in 1967 when Padstow's lifeboat was re-located further westwards along the coast at Mother Ivey's Bay.

**Round Hole**
This unusual chasm was formed by the roof collapse of a sea-cave, the lower section of which was steadily undermined by storm waves.

**Porthmissen Bridge**
The cliffs of this area are composed of altered slates that are over 350 million years old. They give rise to many remarkable features, including Porthmissen Bridge, with its through cave, the Lower, Middle and Higher Meropes, which are rocky sea stacks separated by the narrow Tregudda Gorge, and the fascinating Marble Cliffs, which are composed of limestone alternating with bands of shale.

## PADSTOW 'OBBY 'OSS

Padstow celebrates one of the great May Day festivals with its ceremony of the 'Obby 'Oss, when a great hooped mask, painted and plumed and representing a stylised horse with trailing black skirts, is danced madly round the crowded streets led on by a 'teazer' with a painted club. Those carrying the 'Oss change places regularly, usually outside the packed pubs. The crazily dancing 'Oss is followed by crowds of locals. The style is medieval, the atmosphere electric as the 'Oss chases off men with its wooden 'snappers' and tries to capture girls beneath its skirts. Musicians accompany the 'Oss from dawn to dusk, playing the repetitive, haunting and exciting 'Obby 'Oss May Song. The custom, an ancient fertility rite, was once banned, but was reinstated earlier this century. Do not expect a quiet day, for 'Summer is icumen in...'

*Padstow's harbour has silted up, but it is still a popular refuge for pleasure boats and trawlers*

## PADSTOW   Map ref SW9175

Padstow is a likeable, good-natured town in a fine position on the Camel Estuary. Its maritime history is a noble one, though it was often tragic. The shifting sand bar across the mouth of the estuary, the Doom Bar, is extremely dangerous at certain states of the tide and in heavy seas. Records show that over 300 vessels were wrecked here between 1760 and 1920. At low tide, a vast expanse of sand sweeps away from Padstow, shading to gold towards the sea and to honey-coloured mud towards the inner estuary and Little Petherick Creek. At high tide it is all glittering water, town and estuary on a more level plane. Padstow's busy harbour has been modernised, but in keeping with traditional style. The buildings that cluster around it have great variety, and the maze of streets and narrow passageways behind it are pleasantly cool on sunny mornings.

Padstow was a busy trading port from the earliest times, and Welsh and Irish saints of the Dark Ages landed here. St Petroc arrived from Wales in the 6th century and stayed for 30 years, founding a monastery which thrived until 981 when it was destroyed by marauding Vikings. The present Church of St Petroc is pleasantly sombre within its shaded churchyard. The route of the old railway line, closed in 1967, is now the Camel Trail (see page 48), a walking and cycle route. North of Padstow is Stepper Point the fine headland at the entrance to the estuary. (See Walk on page 42).

The Saints' Way, *Forth an Syns* in Cornish, is a 28-mile (45km) walking route from Padstow to Fowey. It is a delightful route that can be walked in two days and is best started at St Petroc's Church, Padstow. The first part of the route to Little Petherick, 2 miles (3.2km) south of Padstow is worth doing for its own sake. Signposting throughout is generally good; the motif of a stylised Celtic Cross is used on wooden posts.

### TINTAGEL Map ref SX0588

Tintagel should not be missed, even if a visit is fleeting. The focus of this relentlessly 'themed' village is the ruined castle moulded to the blunt summit of 'the Island' of Tintagel Head and approached across a narrow neck of land. The castle is 13th century, but the romance of the site has attracted competing claims for its origins: Iron-Age enclosure, Celtic monastery, Roman signal station and, of course, the court of King Arthur. It is easy to become embroiled in the debate. The French derivation of the name Tintagel is said to be 'stronghold of the Devil', thus letting everyone in on the act. The prominence of the Island, suggests that it was used as a defensive site from the earliest times. The castle and its surroundings are impressive although popularity may elbow out the effect.

Barras Nose to the north and Glebe Cliff to the south, are in the care of the National Trust. It is tempting to say that the hinterland is in the care of the King Arthur industry, but Tintagel village offers much more than that. The wonderfully antiquated Old Post Office (National Trust) at the heart of the village is a delightful building. It is actually a small 14th-century manor house, with a central hall rising the full height of the building, and became a post office only in Victorian times. King Arthur's Great Halls in Fore Street is a remarkable token of dedication to a theme. The building was completed in the early 1930s and is devoted to Arthurian memorabilia and includes a collection of stained-glass windows.

*Tintagel Castle, on its steep headland, is battered by the elements*

#### THE CORNISH PASTY

Traditionally the Cornish pasty was the ideal 'meal-in-one' for miners, farm workers and quarrymen – conveniently packaged and robust enough to be still in one piece by 'croust' or 'crib' time, as meal breaks are known here. True 'pasty paste' is shortcrust with less fat than usual. A mix of chuck steak, potatoes, turnip, and onion is the traditional filling, though vegetable, egg and bacon or even apple pasties, were just as common. The crimped crest of the pasty was often a work of art and a sign of its maker. Initials were marked on one corner of pasties and eaten last, so some could be left for later. Many Cornish bakers still produce good versions.

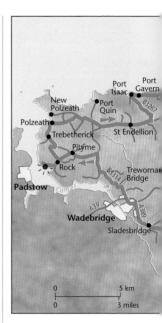

# Bodmin Moor and the North Coast

This 78-mile (125km) drive takes in the wildest and loveliest parts of Bodmin Moor, with a visit to the north coast by way of contrast. The Minions area is dominated by ruined mine engine houses, Cheesewring Quarry and by the rounded bulk of Caradon Hill, while the fine granite ridge of Rough Tor (pronounced 'Row Tor') dominates the western side of Bodmin Moor. The moorland slopes have numerous prehistoric remains of Bronze Age circles and field boundaries.

### ROUTE DIRECTIONS

See Key to Car Tours on page 120.

Leave Launceston on the A388 signed 'Bodmin'. Pass under the main A30 flyover, then, at the next roundabout, take the third exit, signed 'South Petherwin B3254'. Pass through South Petherwin and continue along the B3254 to reach a crossroads with the B3257 at Congdon's Shop. Go straight across and continue for 4½ miles (7.2km), passing through Middlewood and Darleyford, to reach a crossroads at Upton Cross. Turn right onto an unclassified road, signed 'Minions, Siblyback Lake'. Pass through Minions, (parking for moorland walks). Keep ahead at the next junction, signed 'St Cleer', passing an access road on the right to **Siblyback Water Park** (parking, toilets), part of a country park that incorporates Colliford Lake. There is a seasonal exhibition at the Siblyback Visitor Centre.

Continue on the main route, passing **King Doniert's Stone** on the left (parking). At the next junction, turn right, signed 'Draynes, Golitha Falls'. About 300 yards (274.3m) along the road, a left turn over a bridge leads to the car park for Golitha Falls, which lie within a National Nature Reserve. On the main route continue to Bolventor. At a junction turn left, pass the famous **Jamaica Inn**, then turn left opposite the Inn, signed 'Dozmary

*Old slate cottages crowd the beach at Port Isaac*

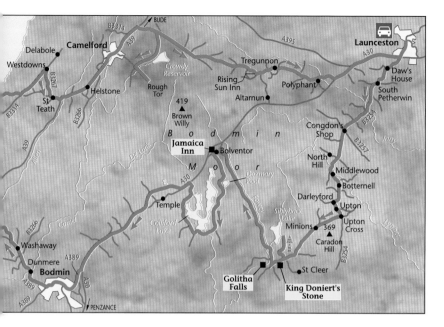

Pool'. Pass Dozmary Pool on the left and continue past Colliford Dam, (parking). At the next junction turn right, signed 'Bodmin'. Continue past lakeside car parks and reach the A30. Turn left, signed 'Bodmin'.

After 7 miles (11.2km), bear left onto the A389, signed 'Bodmin'. Keep ahead for Bodmin, then turn right at a junction, signed 'Bodmin A389'. Go through Bodmin following signs for Wadebridge, A389. At a junction, turn right by a memorial clock tower, signed 'Wadebridge' and continue along the A389 for 6 miles (9.6km). Follow a sign for Padstow, and at a big round-about take the exit signed 'Rock, Polzeath'. Turn right at the next roundabout onto the B3314, signed 'Rock, Polzeath'. Cross the Treworwan Bridge, then after 2 miles (3.2km) turn left, signed 'Rock, Trebetherick'. Continue for 2 miles (3.2km), then opposite a garage turn

right into Trewint Lane, signed 'Trebetherick, Polzeath'. (Detour to Rock here for splendid views across the Camel Estuary).

On the main route, turn left at the next junction, signed 'Trebetherick, Polzeath'. Pass through Trebetherick and descend steeply into Polzeath, then ascend even more steeply. In 1¼ miles (2km) pass a turn-off to New Polzeath. Pass a left turn to Portquin, then keep left off the bend, signed 'St Endellion, Port Isaac'. Soon join the B3314 and go left. Continue for about 2½ miles (4km), passing through St Endellion, then turning left onto the B3267, signed 'Port Isaac'. Go through the upper part of Port Isaac, (park here to visit the village – toilets), and then descend steeply to Portgaverne. Ascend steeply, then continue for 2¼ miles (3.6km) to meet the B3314. Turn left, signed 'Delabole', and continue for 1¾ miles (2.8km) to a junction with the

B3267. Turn right, signed 'St Teath'. Keep ahead through St Teath, signed 'Camelford'. Descend steeply to a T-junction with the A39 and turn left, signed 'Bude, Camelford'. Continue for 3 miles (4.8km) to Camelford.

Go through Camelford and continue along the A39 for about 2 miles (3.2km), then turn right, signed 'Roughtor, Altarnun, Crowdy Reservoir'. After a mile (1.6km) turn right, signed 'Roughtor, Crowdy Reservoir', and follow the road, passing Crowdy Reservoir. At a crossroads, turn left, and soon reach a car park below the impressive granite ridge of Rough Tor. Return to the crossroads, turn right, repass Crowdy Reservoir, then, at a junction, turn right. Continue for about 4 miles (6.4km) to pass the Rising Sun Inn. Keep left and continue direct, ignoring all side roads. After 3½ miles (5.6km) pass Polyphant and reach the A30. Turn left and return to Launceston.

**THE CAMEL TRAIL**
The route of the old Atlantic Coast Express, from Wadebridge to Padstow, is now the main part of the Camel Trail, a walking, riding and cycling route alongside the River Camel through varied countryside. The trail can be joined at Padstow, Wadebridge and at Boscarne Junction to the west of Bodmin, where it swings north to continue through Hellandbridge to terminate at Poley's Bridge. The full extent of the Trail is 16 miles (26km).

*Wadebridge was an early terminal, in 1834, on the railway line from Bodmin*

**WADEBRIDGE**  Map ref SW9972
The estuary of the River Camel narrows to a river's width at Wadebridge. The town was at the head of navigation of the Camel and was a busy port into the early part of the 20th century. The old bridge dates from the mid-15th century and is said to have been built on foundations of woolpacks, the area being noted for its wool production. The bridge has been modified since but it still has a sturdy traditional style. To the west, modern technology has spanned the wider estuary with a lofty road bridge that has eased much of the town's traffic problem. The Camel Trail passes through the town along the track of the old railway.

The small fishing village of Port Isaac lies north of Wadebridge. (See Car Tour on page 46). It is popular and, because the car is effectively sidelined, can perhaps claim to be truly 'unspoiled'. The houses are crowded together with only narrow passageways, called 'drangs', between. The narrowest test-piece is Squeeze Belly Alley, a name that speaks for itself.

**WEST BODMIN MOOR**  Map ref SW1579
Bodmin Moor west of the A30 culminates in the wild and rugged hills of Rough Tor and Brown Willy, the latter the highest point in Cornwall at 1,377 feet (419m). This area is best approached on the A39 from Camelford, home of the North Cornwall Museum and Gallery; an art and craft gallery and Tourist Information Centre are in the same building. To the east, Bodmin Moor begins with a vengeance at the elegant rocky ridge of Rough Tor (pronounced 'Row Tor'), which, at 1,312 feet (400m) deserves to be called a mountain. The climb to the summit is not too daunting, for the fit. This is ancient landscape at its finest, littered with Bronze-Age hut circles and other remains. To the north Showery Tor has fantastic wind-sculpted summit rocks; east is Brown Willy, whose proper name derives from 'bron' for hill and 'ewhella' for highest.

Amidst all this lies the valley of the De Lank River draining southwards past the secretive Garrow Tor and Hawk's Tor. Most of the moorland is grazing common and is privately owned. Dogs should never be let off the leash in the area.

# North Cornwall: Bodmin, Bude, Launceston and Padstow

Leisure Information
Places of Interest
Shopping
Sports, Activities and
the Outdoors
Annual Events and Customs

*Checklist*

## Leisure Information

### TOURIST INFORMATION CENTRES

**Bodmin**
Shire House, Mount Folly Square. Tel: 01208 76616.
**Bude**
The Crescent Car Park. Tel: 01288 354240.
**Camelford**
North Cornwall Museum, The Clease. Tel: 01840 212954. Open weekdays Apr–Sep.
**Launceston**
Market House Arcade, Market Place. Tel: 01566 772321.
**Padstow**
North Quay. Tel: 01841 533449.
**Wadebridge**
Town Hall. Tel: 01208 813725 Open Easter–end Oct.

### OTHER INFORMATION

**Coastguard**
Dial 999 and ask for the Coastguard Service, which co-ordinates rescue service.
**Cornwall Wildlife Trust**
Five Acres, Allet, Truro. Tel: 01872 73939.
**English Heritage**
Portland House, Stag Place, London. Tel: 0171 973 3434.

**Health**
Information on health problems is available Tel: 0800 665544. Dental Helpline Tel: 0800 371192.
**Environment Agency**
Manley House, Kestrel Way, Exeter. Tel: 01392 444000.
**National Trust in Cornwall**
Lanhydrock, Bodmin. Tel: 01208 74281.
**Parking**
Weekly parking tickets are available from pay-and-display machines at North Cornwall District Council's coastal car parks and are interchangeable between coastal car parks.
**Public Transport**
Timetable for bus, coach, rail, ferry and air services in Cornwall is available from Passenger Transport Unit, County Hall, Truro, Tel: 01872 322000.
**South West Water**
Highercombe Park, Lewdown, Okehampton. For enquiries on recreation/fishing Tel: 01837 871565.
**Surf Call**
Report on local surfing conditions. Tel: 0891 333080.
**Weather Call**
South-west weather details. Tel: 0891 500758.

### ORDNANCE SURVEY MAPS

Explorer 1:25,000 Sheets 106, 109, 111, 112. Landranger 1:50,000 Sheets 190, 200.

## Places of Interest

There will be an admission charge at the following places of interest unless otherwise stated.

**Bodmin and Wenford Steam Railway**
General Station, Bodmin. Tel: 01208 73666. Open end May–end Sep, daily; also certain days in winter.
**Bodmin Jail**
Berrycoombe Road, Bodmin. Tel: 01208 76292. Former county prison of the 18th century, complete with cells and dungeons. Exhibition of prison history. Open: all year daily.
**Bodmin Museum**
Mount Folly Square, Bodmin. Tel: 01208 74159. Open Easter–Oct, most days. Free.
**The British Cycling Museum**
The Old Station, Camelford. Tel: 01840 212811. Collection of cycles from early 19th century onwards. Other cycling displays. Open all year, most days.

**Bude–Stratton Museum**
The Old Forge, Lower Wharf, Bude. Tel: 01288 353576. Open Easter–Sep, daily.

**Delabole Slate Quarry**
Pengelly Road, Delabole. Tel: 01840 212242. Open, weekdays (except Bank Hols and 2 weeks Aug). Free.

**Duke of Cornwall's Light Infantry Museum**
The Keep, Bodmin. Tel: 01208 72810. Open weekdays, Bank Hols, and Sun in Jul and Aug.

**John Betjeman Centre**
Southern Way, Wadebridge. Tel: 01208 812392. Collection of memorabilia of the Poet Laureate. Open weekdays except Bank Hol. Free.

**King Arthur's Great Halls**
Fore Street, Tintagel. Tel: 01840 770526. Open all year daily.

**Launceston Castle**
Tel: 01566 772365. Open Apr–Oct, daily.

**Launceston Steam Railway**
St Thomas Road, Launceston. Tel: 01566 775665. Narrow gauge line through Kensey Valley to New Mills. Steam-hauled trains; museum and workshops at station. Open Jun–Sep most days, Apr–May & Oct certain days.

**Lawrence House Museum**
9 Castle Street, Launceston. Tel: 01566 773277. Open Apr to mid-Oct, weekdays.

**Long Cross Victorian Gardens**
St Endellion, near Port Isaac. Tel: 01208 880243. Gardens: open all year; Tavern: open Easter–Oct, daily.

**The Museum of Witchcraft**
The Witches House, Boscastle Harbour. Open Easter–Oct, daily.

**North Cornwall Museum and Gallery**
The Clease, Camelford. Tel: 01840 212954. Open Apr–Sep, most days.

**Old Post Office**
Tintagel. Tel: 01840 770024. Open Apr–Oct, daily.

**Padstow Museum**
Market Place. Padstow's famous 'Obby 'Oss is kept here. Open Easter–Sep, weekdays, Sat mornings.

**Pencarrow House and Gardens**
Washaway, near Bodmin. Tel: 01208 841371. 18th-century house, beautiful gardens and woodland, crafts centre. Open Easter to mid-Oct, most days.

**Prideaux Place**
Padstow. Tel: 01841 532411. Elizabethan house and grounds, formal gardens. Open Easter–Sep, most afternoons.

**The Tamar Otter Sanctuary**
North Petherwin, near Launceston. Tel: 01566 785646. Open Apr–Oct, daily.

**Tintagel Castle**
Tel: 01840 770328. Open all year most days.

The following places may be of interest to visitors with children. Unless otherwise stated there will be an admission charge.

**Donkey Sanctuary (NEDDI)**
Lower Maidenland, St Kew. Between Wadebridge and Camelford. Tel: 01208 841710. Open Sun before Etr–Oct.

**Pixieland Fun Park**
Kilkhampton, near Bude. Tel: 01288 321225. Numerous attractions and activities. Open Apr–Oct, most days.

**Shire Horse Adventure Park**
Trelow Farm, Wadebridge. Tel: 01841 540276. Shire horses, owls, small animals. Open Apr–Oct, daily in high season.

**The Tamar Otter Sanctuary**
North Petherwin, near Launceston. Tel: 01566 785646. Open Apr–Oct, daily.

## Shopping

**Bodmin**
Street market, Mount Folly, Saturday morning.

**Padstow**
Tuesday market (May–Sep).

**Crafts**
The Lower Wharf Gallery, by Bude Canal.

**Pottery**
Boscastle Pottery, The Old Bakery, Boscastle. Tel: 01840 250291.

Port Isaac Pottery, Roscarrock Hill, Port Isaac. Tel: 01208 880625.

Wenford Bridge Pottery, St Breward, Bodmin. Tel: 01208 850471.

## Sports, Activities and the Outdoors

**Sea**
Various trips are available from Padstow harbour; enquire locally for details.

**Coarse**
Tamar Lakes Water Park, near Bude. Permit required.
Crowdy Reservoir, near Camelford Tel: 01837 871565.

**Bude**
Crooklets Beach: popular family beach with good stretch of sand, good surfing. Lifeguard. Dogs not allowed;
Summerleaze: popular family beach. Lifeguard. Dogs not allowed.

**Constantine Bay**
Good sandy area. Limited parking. Lifeguard.

**Crackington Haven**
Pebbly beach with some sand at low tide. Lifeguard. Dogs not allowed.

**Daymer Bay**
Sheltered sandy beach with dunes. Currents can be dangerous at certain times, especially further upriver. Care is advised.

**Harlyn Bay**
Sheltered area of sand and small dunes. Lifeguard.

**Padstow**
On the Camel Estuary north of Padstow. St George's Well and Harbour Cove: these fine beaches are reached on foot from the town and are often quiet. There are no facilities. Care should be taken because of potentially dangerous tidal currents.

**Polzeath, Hayle Bay**
Popular family beach. Lifeguard. Dogs not allowed.

**Trebarwith Strand**
South of Tintagel. Sand and rocks. Lifeguard.

**Trevone Bay**
Pleasant sandy cove. Lifeguard.
Dogs not allowed.
**Treyarnon Bay**
Good family beach. Lifeguard.
**Widemouth**
South of Bude. Long stretch of
flat sand. Good for families and
surfing. Lifeguard. Dogs not
allowed at northern end of
beach.

Lifeguards, where indicated, are
on summer service. Dogs are not
allowed on several popular
beaches from Easter to
September. During winter,
when dogs are allowed, owners
are asked to use poop scoops.

### BOAT TRIPS

**Bude**
Rowing boats and canoes for
hire at Bude Canal.
**Padstow**
Pleasure trips available from the
harbour. Tel: 0836 798457.

### BOWLING

The bowling clubs at Bodmin
and Bude welcome visitors.
Please contact the local Tourist
Information Centre for further
details.

### CYCLING

A network of quiet lanes offers
good cycling between the main
roads and main centres of the
area.

The Camel Trail (see page 48).
Tel: 01208 815631.

Cycling is not permitted on
public footpaths or on the coast
path.

### CYCLE HIRE

**Bodmin**
The Bike Shop, Church Square.
Tel: 01208 72557
**Bude**
North Coast Cycles, Flexbury
Garage, Ocean View Road. Tel:
01288 352974
**Padstow**
Padstow Cycle Hire Ltd, South
Quay. Tel: 01841 533533
**Wadebridge**
Bridge Bike Hire, Eddystone
Road. Tel: 01208 813050.

Camel Trail Cycle Hire,
Trevanson Street. Tel: 01208
814104.
Cycle Revolution, Eddystone
Road. Tel: 01208 812021.

### GOLF COURSES

**Bodmin**
St Kew Golf Club, St Kew
Highway. Tel: 01208 841500.
**Bude**
Bude and North Cornwall Golf
Club, Burn View. Tel: 01288
352006.
**Camelford**
Bowood Golf Club, Lanteglos.
Tel: 01840 213017.
**Launceston**
Launceston Golf Club, St
Stephens. Tel: 01566 773442.
Trethorne Golf Club, Kennards
House. Tel: 01566 86324.
**Padstow**
Trevose Golf and Country Club,
Constantine Bay. Tel: 01841
520208.

### HORSE-RIDING

**Bodmin**
Denby Riding Stables,
Nanstallon. Tel: 01208 72013.
**Boscastle**
Tredole Trekking, Trevalga,
Boscastle. Tel: 01840 250495.
**Bude**
Maer Stables, Crooklets. Tel:
01288 354141.
**Launceston**
Elm Park Equestrian Centre,
North Beer, Boyton. Tel: 01566
785353.
St Leonard's Equestrian Centre,
Polson. Tel: 01566 775543.

*Mayday celebrations at
Padstow with the famous
'Obby 'Oss'*

### SAILING

Camel School of Sailing, Rock.
Tel: 01208 862881.

### WATERSPORTS

**Bude**
Outdoor Adventure, Widemouth
Bay. Tel: 01288 361312.
**Polzeath**
Surfs Up, Polzeath. Tel: 01208
862003.

## Annual Events and Customs

**Bodmin**
Riding Day and Heritage Day.
First Sat in July. Processions,
dances and street stalls.
**Bude**
Jazz Festival. One week at end of
August.
**Padstow**
May Day Festival. Celebration
with famous Padstow 'Obby
'Oss. Very lively and busy.
**Wadebridge**
Royal Cornwall Show. Thu–Sat
in early June. The county's top
agricultural show.

The checklists give details of just
some of the facilities within this
guide. Further information can
be obtained from Tourist
Information Centres.

# Mid Cornwall: Truro, Newquay and Mevagissey

Mid Cornwall is where the county grows ever narrower between the Atlantic and the English Channel and where there is a dramatic contrast between the north and south coasts. The north coast is famous for surfing beaches like those at Newquay and for delightful family beaches backed by sand dunes and flanked by magnificent headlands. The south is more placid, its beaches quieter and pleasantly remote and where, around Mevagissey and the exquisite Roseland Peninsula, there is a lusher quality to the landscape. In the east is St Austell and Cornwall's famous white 'Alps' of the clay country, and at the heart of the region is Truro, cathedral city and busy shopping centre.

### CREME DE LA CREME

The cream tea has a long history. In its various forms there are subtle differences but the Cornish naturally consider their Cream Tea the finest of all. Clotted cream, known originally as 'scald' cream, was made by leaving a pan, containing several pints of fresh milk, to stand overnight. The pan was then placed on the stove to 'scald' and when nearly boiling, was removed to the larder and again left overnight. The resultant creamy yellow crust was then skimmed off. Cornish cream should not be too fluid, nor too thick, but should fall enticingly from the spoon. The proper ritual is to first spread jam on two halves of a Cornish 'split' then to top off with clotted cream.

### BEDRUTHAN STEPS  Map ref SW8468

Access to the beach at Bedruthan has been difficult over the years because of the crumbling nature of the cliffs, but the National Trust has built a secure stairway from the cliff top at Carnewas. The famous 'Steps' are the weathered rock stacks that stand in bold isolation amidst the sand. Bedruthan Steps are the result of sea erosion on the caves and arches in the friable slate cliffs. They have colourful local names, such as Queen Bess, Samaritan Island and Diggory's Island. According to local legend, a mythical giant, Bedruthan, was reputed to use the great stacks as stepping stones; but to nowhere in particular it seems. There is a National Trust shop and café on the cliff top in what was once the office building of the old Carnewas iron mine. Cream teas and other Cornish delights are the order of the day.

## CAMBORNE  Map ref SW6440

Camborne is not picturesque and would not thank you for saying otherwise. Camborne has born the brunt of Cornish industrialisation and of the strip development that the linear shape of the county dictated, but the town thrives still and has Cornwall's last working tin mine, South Crofty, on its doorstep. There are gems of industrial archaeology at Pool, midway between Camborne and Redruth, where the National Trust has restored two great steam engines. Pool also has a geology museum within the Camborne School of Mines, which has many fine rock specimens, including some from Africa, Australia and North and South America. Such a varied collection reflects the influence of Cornish miners on every part of the world where hard rock mining was carried out. There is an art gallery attached to the museum.

Camborne was associated with the greatest of Cornish inventors, Richard Trevithick (1771–1833), a statue of whom stands outside Camborne Public Library in Trevenson Street. Trevithick was born at nearby Illogan. He married a daughter of the Hayle foundry family, the Harveys, and devoted his life to industrial invention and development. Trevithick designed steam engines and invented a steam threshing machine, an early road vehicle, and the first railway engine. Camborne celebrates its famous son with a special Trevithick Day in April. A small museum in the library has displays on mining and archaeology and on Trevithick's work. The nearby Tehidy Country Park (see Walk on page 54) has leafy walks, streams and an ornamental lake, and is close to the breezy north coast.

### COUSIN JACK: THE CORNISH MINER ABROAD

There is a threadbare cliché which says that at the bottom of a deep mine anywhere in the world, you will find a Cornish miner digging even deeper. There is some truth in this. It was the thousands of miners forced into emigration by mining slumps at home, that made the Cornish so famous abroad. A particularly severe slump in copper mining during the 1860s caused many miners to emigrate to The Americas, South Africa and Australia. 'Cousin Jacks', as they were known either sent money home or brought their families to join them, and Cornish names and traditions still survive in far-flung places.

*Below: the engineer Richard Trevithick was a pioneer of the Industrial Revolution*

*Opposite: stacks like giant stepping-stones cross the bay at Bedruthan*

# Sea Cliffs and Shady Woods

*A walk of delightful contrasts that threads its way through peaceful mixed woodland and then along grassy downs above dramatic sea cliffs. Especially fine for woodland flowers during spring and summer. An easy route, with only a few inclines in the woods. The woodland paths may be muddy.*

Time: 2 hours. Distance: 3 miles (4.8km).
Location: 7½ miles (12.1km) north-east of Hayle.
Start: Large parking area on North Cliffs, Reskajeage Downs, just off the B3301 between Hayle and Portreath.
(OS grid ref: SW625431).
OS Maps: Explorer 104 (Redruth & St Agnes) 1:25,000
Landranger 203 (Land's End, The Lizard and Isles of Scilly) 1:50,000.
See Key to Walks on page 121.

## ROUTE DIRECTIONS

From the entrance of the car park cross the road and the stile opposite then walk down the left-hand edge of two fields, keeping left near the

*A springtime carpet of bluebells in Tehidy Woods*

bottom of the second field where the path passes between hawthorn trees. On reaching a road, turn left then after 150 yards (137m), at a right-hand bend, bear off left and pass behind a cottage. Keep ahead along a tree-lined path that soon becomes a broad track, and shortly enter the old Tehidy estate (Tehidy Country Park).

Proceed along a broad drive, then after a quarter of a mile (0.4km), turn right down some wooden steps beside wooden railings, cross a footbridge and follow a boardwalk known as Snake Bridge (slippery when wet). Proceed uphill and at a T-junction turn left and follow a surfaced track through part of **Tehidy's Oak Wood**. Where this track merges with a track from the right, keep ahead, bearing left to reach Otter Bridge signpost. Diversion: an attractive ornamental lake can be reached from here by turning right along a broad track for about a quarter of a mile (0.4km). Dogs, other than guide dogs, are not permitted in the lake area.

Back on the main route, keep ahead past the signpost, cross a stream, then climb a steep and stony section of track to a T-junction. Turn right at Kennels Hill signpost, then bear immediately left, arrowed North Cliff Car Park. Bear left uphill on a track through trees, then at a

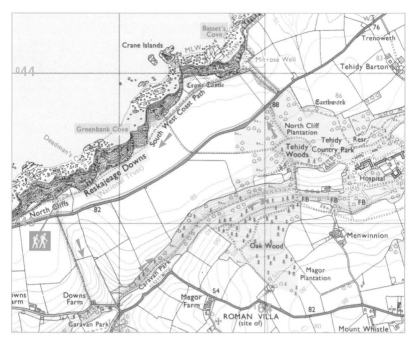

T-junction with a broad track, turn right, and keep right at the next junction. After 100 yards (91m) turn left and go up a broad track to enter the car park.

Go through the car park, to the road, turn right, then after 50 yards (45m) cross the road and turn left down a broad track to reach a large stony area on the cliff top above **Basset's Cove**. You can stop to take in the distant views towards Godrevy lighthouse from this point.

Join the coast path at the bottom left-hand corner of the stony area. The coast path follows the flat unprotected edge of steep cliffs. Take care of children here. Pass the low mound of Crane Castle on the cliff edge, then after a quarter of a mile (0.4km), go through a kissing-gate and proceed along the cliff path above **Greenbank Cove**, and eventually arrive back at the car park.

## POINTS OF INTEREST

### Reskajeage Downs
This windswept area of cliff top represents a wave-cut platform shaped by the higher sea levels of over 350 million years ago. Today, a large part of the area is pasture, but the heathland sections are noted for their wild flowers, many of them being salt-resistant species such as the white bell-like bladder campion, the ubiquitous thrift, and the taller valerian with its pinkish-red flowers.

### Tehidy Woods
This fine estate was once the property of a famous Cornish family, the Bassets, whose ownership dated from Elizabethan times. The estate is now a Country Park covering 250 acres, much of it being delightful woodland. The Oak Wood has a good mix of trees including sessile and pedunculate oak, sweet chestnut, beech, Scots pine, holly, and rhododendron.

### Basset's Cove
The large area of cleared ground above Basset's Cove reflects industrialisation of last century, when the slate and shale cliffs surrounding the cove were quarried for building and road material.

### Greenbank Cove
The general instability of the cliffs along this section of coast has led to quite substantial erosion over the years. The cliffs above Greenbank Cove collapsed some time during the last century and formed a landslip undercliff that enabled easier access to the shore down still surviving mule and donkey tracks. The insignificant mound of Crane Castle was once part of an Iron-Age promontory enclosure.

### BLACK HEAD

Black Head lies south of Charlestown, adding a fine flourish to the southern edge of St Austell Bay. The headland is small but gives fine views and can be reached via an unclassified road off the A390 to Trenarran. From here, it is an easy walk to the headland, with its earthworks of an Iron-Age site. The rifle range on the approach is used only on occasional Sundays in winter, at which time red warning flags are displayed.

*A perfect Georgian port, Charlestown has proved to be a popular backdrop for film-makers*

### CHARLESTOWN  Map ref SX0351

Charlestown is St Austell's gateway to the sea. The port was a late 18th-century creation by local entrepreneur Charles Rashleigh (see page 17) and became known familiarly as 'Charles's town'. The harbour was originally West Polmear, a modest fishing cove where ships ran on to the beach to load copper ore and china clay from the developing industries of the St Austell area. Rashleigh commissioned Eddystone Lighthouse engineer John Smeaton to build a deep harbour with lock gates. The port was very successful.

The road to Charlestown, called, not surprisingly Charlestown Road, is a fine broad avenue in keeping with the breadth of Rashleigh's ambition. Square-rigged ships, including a replica of Columbus's *Santa Maria* are now berthed in the harbour and can be visited. There is a Shipwreck and Heritage Centre and nautical pubs include the Rashleigh Arms of course.

Charlestown is a great favourite with film-makers, and its harbour and handsome sailing ships have been used in *Poldark*, *The Onedin Line* and *The Eagle Has Landed*.

## CRANTOCK  Map ref SW7960

Crantock stands beside the long narrow estuary of the River Gannel, a clear, gliding stream that runs between banks of sand and mud. In the centre of Crantock the serene little Round Garden is now in the care of the National Trust, and the village has two holy wells, one in the centre, the other on the road to the beach. The Church of St Carantocus has been added to and rebuilt over the years but has 13th- and 14th-century features. There are shops and pubs in the village, and a tea-garden that is open during the summer months. Crantock beach lies just a little way to the west of the village; above the beach is Rushy Green, an area of sand dunes.

To the west of Crantock is West Pentire, where there is a car park. From here you can take the zigzag track south to Porth Joke, also known as Polly Joke – a jolly name for a charming sand-filled cove.

Holywell Bay lies further south again and is reached from Crantock by following an unclassified road south to Cubert, from where a right turn leads to the car park above Holywell's sandy beach.

**ANCHORING THE SANDS**

The partnership between the shifting sands and marram grass is remarkable. Little will grow in this dry, constantly moving environment, but marram grass thrives on it, being stimulated into growth of up to a metre a year the more the sands are blown around. In return, the marram traps the sand between its stems and this eventually stabilises the land. Then the marram dies back allowing other plants to flourish.

*Crantock church*

*The light on Godrevy Island, built in 1859, is said to have inspired Virginia Woolf's novel* **To The Lighthouse**

## GODREVY HEAD   Map ref SW5842

The National Trust property of Godrevy Head stands at the eastern end of St Ives Bay and is the first of a sequence of high rugged cliffs of dark slate that run uninterruptedly to the north-east. Offshore from the headland stands Godrevy Island and its crowning lighthouse. There is ample parking at Godrevy Head on grassy downs that are reached along a winding road. Paths lead across and around the headland; the off-shore waters attract inquisitive Grey seals. To the south lies Gwithian Beach, and inland is the village of Gwithian where there is a handsome church and an attractive pub.

## GORRAN HAVEN AND THE DODMAN
Map ref SX0141

Gorran Haven lies just south of Mevagissey at the seaward end of a shallow valley. Steep lanes and passageways climb from the harbour and an intriguing little chapel built on solid rock dates from the 15th century. South of Gorran Haven, the mighty Dodman Point thrusts its bull's head into the seaway. The Dodman, as it is commonly known, is 373 feet (114m) high, an impressive leap from sea-level. It has a strange, lonely atmosphere and, although it dominates the coast, its summit is unspectacular because it is so broad and flat. In keeping with the scale of the great headland, the Iron-Age earthworks that enclose the seaward area of the Dodman are over 2,000 feet (609m) long and 20 feet (6m) high. The embankment is known as the Baulk or Bulwark. The Dodman is crowned by a rather grim stone cross erected by a late Victorian vicar as an aid to navigators.

**HELL AND DEADMAN**
Just east of Godrevy Head and close to the B3301 is the awesome Hell's Mouth, a vast gulf in the cliff where wind and waves are steadily eroding the softer sedimentary rock of a faultline. The view is unnerving but is conveniently enjoyed because it is close to the road. Further east lies Deadman's Cove, another gruesomely named venue.

## MEVAGISSEY  Map ref SX0144

Mevagissey tucks into the land and guards itself within the folded arms of its inner and outer harbours. It became a leading pilchard fishing port in Tudor times and continued as such into this century. For many years it supplied the navy with pilchards, which became known as Mevagissey Ducks. Today there is still a fishing fleet here but one that is more diverse. Like most Cornish fishing villages Mevagissey has great character, especially in the old part of the village that lies between the Fountain Inn and the Battery on the eastern side of the harbour. Many of the houses are pleasingly colour-washed and though the harbour area has seen some rather brutal modern development, the village has retained its Cornish charm.

The inner harbour is a place to linger on warm summer days – seats line the quays but competition is fierce. The narrow alleys and streets of the village draw you on to the next corner, past galleries and gift shops and in and out of light and shade. An aquarium at the old lifeboat house on the South Quay gives an insight into life in deeper waters (the profits go to the upkeep and improvement of Mevagissey harbour). There is a fine little museum of local history on the East Quay and, engagingly for this sea-going town, there is a model railway museum in Meadow Street.

Heligan Garden, with emphasis on the middle syllable please, was a lost garden that has been well and truly found. It lies north-west of Mevagissey and can be reached from the B3273 St Austell road. For decades this magnificent 19th-century garden, complete with classical features, walled gardens and kitchen garden, was lost beneath shrouds of laurel, ivy and bramble. It is the largest garden restoration scheme in Europe and the project is continuing. The results so far are outstanding and include an Italian Garden, and an extensive valley garden with a splendid collection of tree ferns.

### THE LOST GARDENS OF HELIGAN

The story of the 'lost' gardens of Heligan is compelling. From 1780 onwards, the Tremaynes developed 57 acres of their property at Heligan as a series of splendid gardens. Nature began to get a hold on the gardens during World War I, when the house became a military convalescent home and most of the 22 gardeners enlisted. The house was used again by the American military during World War II and was later converted into flats, and though the Tremaynes still owned the gardens, they remained untouched. In 1990 the estate was inherited by John Willis who, with others, made tentative inroads into the impenetrable jungle and discovered the intact framework of a magnificent garden. By Easter 1992 parts of Heligan were open to the public and by the end of 1995 most of the restoration was complete.

*Houses are built into the impossibly steep hillside above Mevagissey harbour*

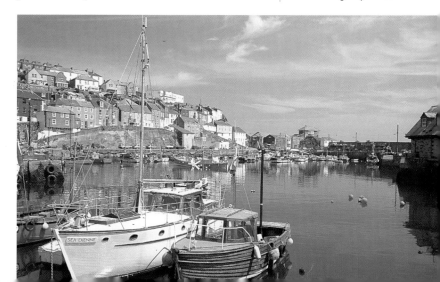

# High Headland and Flower-filled Valley

*An airy stroll round the high promontory of Nare Head that stands between Gerrans Bay and Veryan Bay on Cornwall's sheltered south coast. The wooded sections are especially beautiful in spring and summer. A few inclines and a steep climb and descent at Tregagle's Hole. The field paths can be very muddy.*

Time: 2½ hours. Distance: 3 miles (4.8km).
Location: 13 miles (20.9km) south-east of Truro.
Start: Carne Beach car park, situated 1 mile (1.6km) off the
A3078 between St Mawes and Tregony, 1 mile (1.6km) from
Veryan. (OS grid ref: SW905384).
OS Maps: Explorer 105 (Falmouth & Mevagissey) 1:25,000
Landranger 204 (Truro and Falmouth) 1:50,000.
See Key to Walks on page 121.

## ROUTE DIRECTIONS

Leave the car park by its entrance lane and turn left up the road. Just round a steep bend, bear right up a flight of steps, then go through a kissing gate and continue along the field edge. Go over a stone stile, then bear left and uphill by a signpost. Follow a path through gorse bushes steeply uphill to a field gate at the top of the slope. Turn right at the gate, follow a grassy path to reach a further gate at a very wet area. Proceed along a track for 50 yards (46m) to a junction of tracks just before Carne and turn right, signed 'Nare Head'. Descend and rejoin the coast path.

Head south-east with fine views of Nare Head then climb steeply to a stile into a field. Follow the path right and then descend downhill into Paradoe Cove above **Tregagle's Hole**. Note the

ruined cottage.

Cross a footbridge over a stream, climb a few yards, then, abreast of the ruin, turn left at a signpost and follow a grassy track rising inland through lovely woodland for about a third of a mile (0.5km) to a stile. Turn left along the field edge to another stile and enter a small car park below **Pennare Wallas** farm.

Cross the lane at the entrance to the car park, climb a stile by a National Trust sign for Kiberick Cove and head straight down the field for a short distance, before turning right along the coast path through muddy, broken ground. Go through a gap, then keep uphill towards a fence on the skyline. Continue along the coast path overlooking the island of **Gull Rock**. At a fence corner, turn right over a stile bear left alongside the wire fence and

proceed round the vast gulf of Rosen Cliff. Climb a stile and cross an open grassy area passing between the grassed-over mound of a World War II bunker and the ventilators of a Royal Observer Corps underground station.

Continue along a broad muddy track between thick gorse. Soon, the ground opens out beyond where a wire fence on the right makes a sharp right turn. (Dogs should be kept on leads in this area, where sheep often graze.) Proceed ahead, away from the wire fence, and follow the edge of the gorse on the left to reach an acorn signpost in a dip. (A track going left from here leads out to the rocky summit of **Nare Head**.) Follow the edge of the rough ground over the brow of the hill to a signpost, then steeply descend to Tregagle's Hole and Paradoe Cove. Ascend steeply out of the cove and remain on the coast path all the way back to Carne Beach and the car park.

## POINTS OF INTEREST

**Tregagle's Hole**
This is the name given to a through-cave in a rock outcrop in Paradoe Cove, the small bay in the lee of Pennarin Point. Tregagle, or Tregeagle, was a mythical giant who is said to have played quoits with the outcrops of quartzite that are common throughout the area. More interestingly, the ruined cottage on the cliff was lived in by a fisherman called Mallet who, during the early part of the 19th century, worked a small boat from the small inlet below, called Mallet's Cove.

**Pennare Wallas**
The valley leading up to the car park has been re-planted with white poplar, sweet

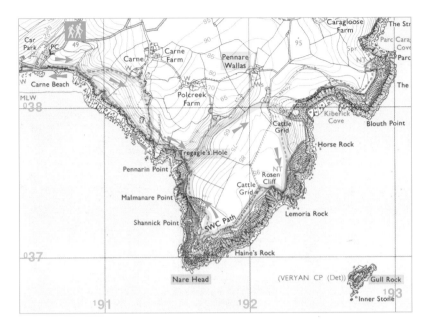

chestnut, sycamore and various conifers. Daffodils, primroses and bluebells fill the valley in spring.

**Gull Rock**
For centuries Gull Rock was used as a source of food in the form of eggs and seabirds. It is now a key breeding site for numerous birds including kittiwake, guillemots and cormorants.

**Nare Head**
The hard pillow lava here has resisted erosion and projects between Gerrans Bay and Veryan Bay. It has a flattened profile, but its seaward side is satisfyingly steep and rocky. The great gulf of Rosen Cliff is very impressive.

*Looking out to Gull Rock from Nare Head*

## CHEATING THE DEVIL

Veryan has five thatched round houses – two at either end of the village and one at its heart, and each is crowned with a cross. They were built during the early 19th century, perhaps on a whim, although local legend claims that their circular form was planned so as to cheat the devil of corners to hide in. Veryan has two holy wells to complete the exorcism. You can't help wondering why all this was necessary.

## MYLOR   Map ref SW8135

Between Truro and Falmouth is the parish of Mylor, dense with trees and bordered by tidal creeks. A network of country lanes north of Falmouth links Mylor Bridge, Mylor Churchtown, Restronguet Passage and Mylor Creek. There was once a royal dockyard at Mylor Churchtown where, during the 19th century, the Falmouth packet ships that delivered mail world-wide were repaired and victualled. The Church of St Mylor is in a superb position and has some unique features – a turret rises from its west gable and it has Norman doorways and a fine interior. The gravestones of Mylor are instructive and entertaining. The headstones of Joseph Crapp, near the east window, and of Thomas James, smuggler, near a fork in the churchyard path, bring a smile to your face. Due south from Mylor Bridge is the attractive village of Flushing, its face to Falmouth just across the river, and a passenger ferry links the two.

## NARE HEAD   Map ref SW9136

Nare Head is the focus of a beautiful stretch of coast that borders the parishes of Gerrans, Veryan and St Michael Caerhays, between the Roseland Peninsula and Dodman Point. The easiest approach to the area is along the A3078 then by an unclassified road that leads to the village of Veryan, noted for its unique and elegant church and for its remarkable thatched round houses. The Church of St Symphorian is impressive, with a dark tower of mottled stone, and is surrounded by shrubs and trees. There are a number of beaches along the shores of Gerrans Bay and Veryan Bay. The best beaches are at Pendower and Carne where there is good parking and access to Nare Head (see Walk on page 60). To the east is the quiet little village of Portloe which has a small car park at its eastern end. Further east again is a beach at Porthluney below Caerhays Castle, a 19th-century picturesque replacement for an older building.

*Small boats rest in the mud at low tide in Mylor Creek*

## NEWQUAY  Map ref SW8161

Newquay is too often described, with a hint of unjustified disparagement, as the Llandudno or the Margate of Cornwall. The town is geared unashamedly to its splendid beaches, of course, and in places there seem to be more hotels and guest houses than breathing space. But Newquay was once Porth Lystry, the 'boat beach', and its harbour, or 'new quay', dates from 1439 when it was decided that it would be a safer landing place for vessels than the Gannel Estuary. The Gannel had been used for years, but was dangerous in Atlantic swells. Business at Newquay was brisk, with much pilchard fishing, and copper and china clay export in later years. Today, at the harbour, there is a strong sense of the 'old' Newquay. Sea-angling trips are available; a good way of appreciating the marine environment and the sea-going traditions of this Cornish town.

Newquay is lively. Broad, busy streets with shops, pubs and clubs and the beaches make the town the epitome of bright and breezy holidaymaking. Yet there are quiet corners in flower-filled parks and gardens. There is a zoo and fun pools and a swimming pool at the Water World in Trenance Leisure Park off Edgcumbe Avenue.

The Elizabethan manor house of Trerice (National Trust) lies just 3 miles (4.8km) south east of Newquay. It is an exquisite building, steadfast, and full of repose, and with some outstanding features. The Hall rises through two storeys and has a lattice window of 576 panes. Several hundred acres of the surrounding manor farm were sold off in lots earlier this century. In 1953 the National Trust bought the house and 20 acres of ground surrounding it. The original Elizabethan gardens had long since disappeared but the Trust has laid out the south side of the old garden with fruit trees in a classic 17th-century pattern of pleasing symmetry. There is a restaurant in the Barn and, in an adjacent hayloft, there is a collection of antique lawnmowers.

**SURF AND SAND**

Newquay's beaches are the most extensive and accessible in Cornwall. They run in a line to the north, from Towan Beach, in front of the town, through Great Western and Tolcarne Beaches to Lusty Glaze and Porth. Further north again is the sweeping expanse of Watergate Bay, all shining sand and glittering sea, with a pause at Berryl's Point, before the popular family beach of Mawgan Porth is reached. The Atlantic swells make Newquay's impressive Fistral Beach a leading surfing venue.

*Newquay's extensive Fistral Beach hosts world-class surfing championships during the summer*

### ST PIRAN'S ORATORY

Perranporth's name derives from St Piran, Cornwall's patron saint, who is credited with bringing Christianity to the county from Ireland during the 6th or 7th century. He built a tiny oratory on Penhale Sands, but though faith may move mountains it cannot bind sand, and the oratory was abandoned to the dunes by the 11th century. A new church was then built further inland, but that too was covered by sand. Both sites can be visited by following the coast path north from Perranporth. There is a stone marker at the site of the oratory and a four-holed circular cross at the site of the church, a short distance further on.

*Sand, sea and fascinating rock features are characteristics of the Cornish coast*

### PERRANPORTH   Map ref SW7554

The Porth of 'Perran' is the small river channel that slices through the sands into Perran Bay. This is real sand country. A great swathe of it runs north from Perranporth and, at low tide especially, offers the exhilarating pleasure of beach walking into the distance. But don't walk too far; because at the northern end of the great beach is a military training area. It is because of the drifting sands here that Perranporth has had three St Piran's churches. The first, dating from the 6th or 7th century, was abandoned as early as the 11th century and, though discovered in the 19th century, has been reburied for its own preservation. The second was abandoned in the 15th century and the latest was sensibly built in a neighbouring village.

Perranporth is a very pleasant resort which has also benefited from being at the heart of 'Poldark Country', a welcome marketing image drawn from the Poldark novels that illustrate what life was like in Cornwall in the late 19th century. Most people will be aware of them from their adaptation into a popular television series. The early books in the saga were written by Winston Graham during the time he lived in Perranporth and many local features inspire the books. He developed his image of the Cornish coastline featured in *Poldark* from a composite of the coast from Perranporth to Crantock, near Newquay. The area of Perranporth itself was the model for Nampara, the fictional district within which the stories are set. Perranporth Beach is the model for Hendrawna Beach that features in the books.

## PORTREATH   Map ref SW6545

Portreath is another part of industrial Cornwall that has weathered its decline and is now being recognised as an important industrial heritage site. The harbour still has the look of a place where coal and copper ore were once shipped through in huge quantities. There are the remains of an incline on which loaded wagons were raised and lowered from the mineral tramroad that connected the port with the mines of St Day, 8 miles (12.9km) away. There is a beach at Portreath and the cliff walks to north and south are worthwhile.

Porthtowan is a small resort lying about 3 miles (4.8km) to the north-east.

## PROBUS   Map ref SW8947

The village of Probus has the tallest church tower in Cornwall. It is over 123 feet (37.5m) high and is lavishly decorated. As if this was not distinction enough Probus also boasts one of Cornwall's most interesting gardens. This is Probus Gardens, a demonstration garden of great variety where much good work is carried out and where keen gardeners can pick up a few tips while they enjoy the varied displays of flowers, shrubs, vegetables and fruit. Probus can be reached along the A390 from Truro or St Austell. The garden is on the St Austell side of the village.

A short distance along the A390 from Probus Gardens is the ornamental Trewithen garden surrounding the handsome 18th-century Trewithen House. The garden is open to the public.

*The long, narrow harbour at Portreath ends in a sheltered pool*

**THE PORTREATH MINERAL TRAMROAD**
The mineral tramroad that linked Portreath to the mines of St Day near Redruth is now an excellent waymarked walk of about 8 miles (12.8km). In parts the route can be used for cycling. It passes through quiet farmland and historic mining country of great interest. An interpretative board at Portreath car park gives details and the route is waymarked.

*Redruth is an important focus for Cornwall's industrial heritage*

**CARN BREA**

Redruth is overlooked by the rocky ridge of Carn Brea, which rises to 740 feet (228m), its long spine punctuated by granite tors. The top of Carn Brea is reached by a rough track from near Carnkie, off the B3297 Helston road. It is believed to have been the site of a Neolithic encampment during the period 4000 to 2500 BC, then Iron-Age occupation from about 500 BC saw the building of a huge walled enclosure (parts of which can still be traced) with over 100 round houses. On top of the hill is a grim monument to local Victorian industrialist Sir Francis Basset. A Gothic folly, now a restaurant, is at the eastern end of the summit ridge. There is a network of paths throughout the area.

**REDRUTH**   Map ref SW6942

Copper and tin mining created Redruth, and then abandoned it. But from the early 18th century until the middle of the 19th, Redruth was the true capital of Cornish mining. Redruth and the mining country that surrounds it is now recognised for the value of its industrial archaeology, and the area has been proposed as a World Heritage Site.

Redruth's association with mining probably dates from the earliest times. In those days the method of tin extraction which would have been used was tin-streaming, whereby tinners sifted through river sand and gravel for fragments of ore. The disturbance caused by tin-streaming released a red stain into rivers and streams and it was this red colour that gave Redruth its engaging name, although in odd reversal of what you would expect: red coming from 'rhyd' for ford, and 'ruth', meaning red.

The town has some interesting architecture including Georgian, Victorian neo-Gothic, and art deco. There is much brickwork and some startling features such as the Italianate clock tower on the corner of Fore Street and Alma Place. Leading off Fore Street is Cross Street where there is a house with an outside staircase, once the home of William Murdock, a Scottish engineer and inventor who worked in Redruth during the late 18th century. Among his many achievements, Murdock developed a lighting system using coal gas, and his house in Cross Street was the first house in the world to be lit in this way (in 1872).

## THE ROSELAND PENINSULA  Map ref SW8536

The name Roseland evokes serenity and colour. This beautiful peninsula seems to have stolen away from the rest of the county; there is a sense of entering another country, a minuscule peninsula, quietly detached from mainstream Cornwall. Flanked on its eastern side by a rock-fringed coast curving north into Gerrans Bay, it is bordered on the west by the River Fal, with Mylor and Feock opposite. The very tip of the Roseland is pierced by the twisting Percuil River that cuts deeply inland to create even smaller peninsulas. The area is famous for the village of St Mawes, for St Mawes Castle and for the Church of St Just-in-Roseland. A pleasant alternative to the main A3078 onto the peninsula, is to take the A39 southwards from Truro, the B3289, past Trelissick Gardens and then cross the Fal by the King Harry Ferry. Another satisfying approach is to take the passenger ferry from Falmouth to St Mawes.

St Just-in-Roseland is an exquisite place, perhaps too accessible for its own good but irresistible. The church stands on the banks of a small creek, its mellowed stonework embedded in a garden of shrubs and graceful trees that include palms as well as indigenous broadleaves.

On the promontory of land between Carrick Roads and the Percuil River stands St Mawes, deservedly popular and besieged with moored yachts in summer. On Castle Point to the west stands Henry VIII's St Mawes Castle, a quiet triumph of good Tudor design over function and praised by Pevsner and the Cornish historian A L Rowse for its symmetry and decoration. You could have no worthier recommendation. On a bright, breezy day of deep blue skies, St Mawes Castle is invigorating rather than menacing. The outer arm of the Roseland terminates at St Anthony Head (one of the National Trust properties on the peninsula) where there is a lighthouse and gun battery with an interesting history. On the east coast, further north, is Portscatho, open-faced to the sea and with good beaches near by.

### ST MAWES FERRIES

There is a regular ferry service between St Mawes and Falmouth, that is worthwhile simply for the pleasure of crossing the Fal Estuary. Another ferry runs the short distance from St Mawes to Place on St Anthony Head, and is a delightful way of visiting the area. A fine circular walk of about 3 miles (4.8km) can be made round St Anthony Head from Place to just above Porthbeor Beach on the south coast; from here a short path links to the road back to Place.

*St-Just-in-Roseland, dating from the 13th to 15th centuries, is beautifully set on a tidal creek*

*The pier at Trevaunance Cove, essential for the loading of ore, was washed away by a storm in 1934*

**CORNISH ENGINE HOUSES**
North of Chapel Porth, standing on a lonely stretch of coastline, is the formidable engine house of the Wheal Coates mine. It is one of many such distinctive buildings which are a feature of the Cornish countryside, and once housed the engine which provided the essential services of winding, pumping and ventilation for the mine. Wheal Coates is an important relic of the county's industrial past, and has been restored by the National Trust, which cares for much of this historic coast. Chapel Porth lies at the heart of old mining country. The coast path to the south leads to Porthtowan through a desolate mining landscape that is also rich in wild flowers.

**ST AGNES**  Map ref SW7150

Mining made St Agnes. Tin and copper ore and lead from nearby mines were exported from here by sea, but it was a difficult coast for seagoing. To either side of Trevaunance Cove below St Agnes the gaunt cliffs made landing by boat difficult. Trevaunance had a small cramped harbour, where coal and other materials had to be raised by a winch and pulley system and the ore tipped down chutes. Since mining ceased in the early years of this century, the sea has made a resort of this charming north coast village. Trevaunance Cove is quite small but it commands the seaward end of St Agnes. The village is easily accessible from the A30 yet seems pleasantly detached from a busier Cornwall. It is a convoluted village with a one-way system that may confuse you at first. A row of picturesque cottages, called Stippy Stappy, leads down from the upper village to the valley below. There is a fine little museum in Penwinnick Road.

West of the village is the shapely hill of St Agnes Beacon, quickly reached by following Beacon Drive to a National Trust parking area on its north side. A good path leads easily to the summit and to magnificent views along the coast to north and south. South of St Agnes is the sandy cove of Chapel Porth.

North of Chapel Porth, and reached along the coast path, are the impressive remains of the engine house of Towanroath, now restored by the National Trust. Dating from 1872, it housed the massive steam engine used to pump water from the nearby Wheal Coates mine.

## ST AUSTELL   Map ref SX0152

Cornwall's famous clay 'Alps' dominate the landscape around St Austell. The town is a good shopping centre, but its outlook is marred by the industrial sprawl that surrounds it – the price of vigorous industry. Even when it was a mere village St Austell was the centre of good farming country, open-cast tin extraction and stone quarrying. Today, the centre of St Austell has been modernised, to some extent in sympathy with its fine traditional buildings. Fore Street and the area around Holy Trinity have been conserved and the Town Hall is in bold Renaissance style, a granite palazzo incorporating a splendid market hall with its interior still intact. The Church of The Holy Trinity has sculpted figures set within niches on all four faces of the impressive tower, which itself is faced with Pentewan stone from the ancient coastal quarries to the south. The pearly-grey stone has a warmer tinge showing through when wet.

The clay country to the north of St Austell overpowers the surrounding area. Here is Cornwall's most startling industrial landscape, from which clay has been extracted on a massive scale. The clay is kaolin, which is decayed granite feldspar. It was once used for making porcelain but is now used mainly in paper-making.

About three million tonnes are produced in the St Austell area annually. Much waste is generated and the great snowy tips have created a strangely compelling landscape. The China Clay Heritage Centre is situated at Carthew to the north of St Austell on the B3274. Further north again is the village of Roche with its adjacent Roche Rock. This remarkable outcrop of quartz schorl, an altered granite, is unique in Cornwall and a startling feature in the midst of the industrial landscape. The only regret is that the area for miles around is not dotted with similar bare pinnacles. The largest outcrop is crowned by the ruins of the ancient chapel of St Michael, which was built in 1409.

**CLAY COUNTRY CIRCUIT**
The vast spoil tips of the St Austell clay country are composed of feldspar and quartz. The raw clay is stripped from the faces of the clay pits by high pressure hoses creating numerous flooded pits throughout the area, their translucent green and blue waters adding to the strange surrealism of this constantly changing 'lunar' landscape. The best way to appreciate the clay country is to drive through it – explore the area north and west of St Austell between the B3279 and the B3274, which takes in Nanpean, Roche, the Roche Rock and the China Clay Heritage Centre at Carthew.

*The 15th-century tower of St Austell's Holy Trinity Church is elaborately worked*

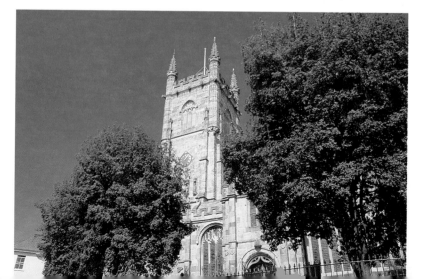

*The charming Gothic bank occupies a strategic corner in St Columb Major*

### ST COLUMB MAJOR   Map ref SW9163

St Columb Major, on high ground 5 miles (8km) east of Newquay, was once traffic-bound but a bypass has eased the congestion in its narrow streets which are enclosed between slate-hung houses. There is some very fine architecture, including an Italianate Gothic building of red and yellow bricks that now houses a bank. Opposite is the attractive Red Lion Inn, and much of the main square dates from the Regency period. The Church of St Columba has a procession arch through the base of its tower. The tower is impressive but has been marred by being rendered with cement in a bid to cure internal dampness, a forlorn hope in sea-washed Cornwall.

#### THE HURLING MATCH

St Columb's fame comes from its annual 'hurling match', held on Shrove Tuesday. Two teams, Townsmen and Countrymen, range widely and wildly, through the town and surrounding countryside in pursuit of a small silver ball which they try to deliver to 'goals', 2 miles (3.2km) apart. This is not cricket. Ground floor windows in the centre of St Columb, where the match begins, are boarded up on the day and on the Saturday of the following week, when the event is repeated.

### TRELISSICK   Map ref SX8339

Trelissick is a beautiful woodland park of some 370 acres, overlooking the Fal Estuary; the house is not open to the public. The grounds were laid out with carriage drives and were planted with trees during the 1820s to take full advantage of the classically picturesque views. The parkland is criss-crossed with pathways which provide some delightful walks.

In the sheltered position that the gardens enjoy, many unusual and exotic plants thrive, including sub-tropical species of fragile beauty from South America and Tasmania. But the gardens are particularly noted for their camellias, magnolias and hydrangeas, of which there are over 100 kinds. The large walled garden has fig trees and climbing plants, and there is a shrub garden. Plants are available in the garden shop and there is an art and craft gallery and a restaurant. Theatrical and musical events are often held at Trelissick.

## TRURO   Map ref SW8244

Truro's great cathedral catches the eye from all quarters. It rises from the heart of the city, its honey-coloured stone and lancet windows reflecting the sun, its great Gothic towers piercing the sky. There is no trace of the Norman castle that once stood at Truro, nor of the Dominican friary that stood near the low ground by the river, but the cathedral makes up for their loss.

Truro's fortunes rose and fell over the years, but by the late 18th century it had become the political and cultural centre of Georgian Cornwall. It was during the last years of the 18th century that such famous features as Boscawen Street and Lemon Street were built. Today Boscawen Street is a broad, cobbled space, entered at both ends from narrow thoroughfares. The granite façade of the City Hall still graces Boscawen Street, and Lemon Street survives as one of the finest examples of a late Georgian street in Britain, its houses perfectly aligned to either side of a broad avenue that climbs gracefully uphill.

There are hidden glories in Truro amidst the cruder modern developments. From the functional harshness of the Moorfield car park, a cramped lane leads to Victoria Square, but parallel and to its right is the elegant Georgian crescent of Walsingham Place. Throughout the heart of Truro alleyways and lanes connect the main streets and are lined with attractive shops, cafés and restaurants. From the west end of Boscawen Street, King Street leads up to the pedestrianised area of High Cross in front of the cathedral. The stylish Assembly Rooms, with a façade of Bath stone, stands near by.

### TRISTAN AND ISEULT

Princess Iseult of Ireland was betrothed to King Mark of Cornwall and on her journey across the Irish Sea to her wedding she was accompanied by Tristan of Lyonesse. But unwittingly they drank a potion which caused them to fall in love with each other. King Mark banished Tristan, who wandered as a minstrel, then married someone else, but he never forgot Iseult and when he was suffering from a poisoned wound, he sent for her (she was known as a skilled healer). In a fit of jealousy, his wife told Tristan that Iseult was not coming and he died broken hearted. When Iseult arrived too late to save him, she too died. His widow repented and buried them together, planting two rose trees, which intertwined over the grave.

*Completed in 1910, Truro's magnificent cathedral is relatively modern*

**WOODLAND WALKS**

Cornwall has wide open spaces to spare. But there are also good areas of woodland in the county. North of Truro, at Idless, is Bishop's Wood, a pleasant Forestry Commission plantation of mainly conifers but with a mix of broadleaved trees such as birch, hazel and willow. The wood can be reached by driving north from Truro on the B3284 to Shortlanesend, from where side roads lead to Idless. There is a car park at the edge of the wood just north of Idless. The wood is criss-crossed with broad forest tracks and there is a pleasant walk alongside a busy little stream.

*The Georgian terraces of Lemon Street, dating from around 1795, should not be missed*

Seen from its forecourt the cathedral seems crowded in by the surrounding buildings, instead of being the dominating presence that commands the view from outside the city. But the west front and its soaring towers is exhilarating. The foundation stones of the cathedral were laid in 1880 and the western towers were finally dedicated in 1920. Truro's cathedral is thus a Victorian building. It is Early English Gothic in design but with strong French influences that are seen in the great spires. The interior is glorious. It is vaulted throughout and pillars and arches are in the most elegant proportion, the air light beneath the great roofs. There are beautiful individual features such as the exquisite baptistry. All that remains of the old parish church of St Mary's is incorporated into the cathedral's south aisle.

Those with an eye for ancient stonework may find the outer wall of the old church a reassuring contrast to the rather smooth planes of the Victorian cathedral. Pydar Street runs north from the cathedral as a pleasant pedestrian concourse but loses its identity at a busy junction. A short distance away is the Crown Court, a stylish building designed by the same architects who were responsible for the St Ives Tate Gallery. Below here are the pleasant Victoria Gardens. Boscawen Park, by the Truro River, is reached along the road to Malpas. The Royal Cornwall Museum in River Street has an excellent collection of minerals and there are exhibitions covering archaeology and mining. The art gallery has works by John Opie, the 18th-century portrait painter who was born near St Agnes. Truro is an excellent shopping centre with numerous shops offering a great variety of quality goods.

# Mid Cornwall: Truro, Newquay and Mevagissey

Leisure Information
Places of Interest
Shopping
The Performing Arts
Sports, Activities and
the Outdoors
Annual Events and Customs

Checklist ✔

## Leisure Information

### TOURIST INFORMATION CENTRES

**Mevagissey**
14 Church Street. Tel: 01726 842266.
**Newquay**
Municipal Buildings, Marcus Hill. Tel: 01637 871345.
**Perranporth**
Perranporth Tel: 01872 573368.
**St Austell**
Bypass Service Station, Southbourne Road.
Tel: 01726 76333.
Seasonal.
**Truro**
Municipal Buildings, Boscawen Street. Tel: 01872 274555.

### OTHER INFORMATION

**Coastguard**
Dial 999 and ask for the Coastguard Service.
**Cornwall Wildlife Trust**
Five Acres, Allet, Truro.
Tel: 01872 73939
**English Heritage**
Portland House, Stag Place, London. Tel: 0171 973 3434.
**Health**
Information on health problems is available Tel: 0800 665544.
Dental Helpline Tel: 0800 371192.

**Environment Agency**
Manley House, Kestrel Way, Exeter. Tel: 01392 444000
**National Trust in Cornwall**
Cornwall Regional Office, Lanhydrock, Bodmin. Tel: 01208 74281
**Parking**
Weekly parking tickets, valid for Restormel District Council car parks, are available from Newquay Tourist Information Centre or from attendants.
**South West Water**
Highercombe Park, Lewdown, Okehampton. For enquiries on recreation and angling
Tel: 01837 871565.
**Surf Call**
Report on local surfing conditions. Tel: 0891 333080.
**Weather Call**
South-west weather details.
Tel: 0891 500758

### ORDNANCE SURVEY MAPS

Explorer 1:25,000 Sheets 104, 105, 106.
Landranger 1:50,000 Sheets 200, 203, 204.

## Places of Interest

There will be an admission charge at the following places of interest unless otherwise stated.

**Automobilia**
The Old Mill, St Stephen, St Austell. Tel: 01726 823092.
Open Apr–Sep, most days.
**Camborne Museum**
Camborne Library, The Cross.
Tel: 01209 713544. Open all year, weekday afternoons, Sat morning. Free.
**Camborne School of Mines Geological Museum**
Pool, Redruth. Tel: 01209 714866. Open weekdays, except Bank Hol. Free.
**Charlestown Shipwreck and Heritage Centre**
Charlestown, near St Austell. Tel: 01726 69897. Open Mar–Oct, daily.
**Cornish Engines**
Pool, near Redruth. Tel: 01209 216657. Open Apr–Oct, daily.
**The Cornish Shire Horse Trust and Carriage Museum**
Lower Gryllis Farm, Treskillard, Redruth. Tel: 01209 713606.
Open Easter–Oct. Closed Sat.
**Folk Museum**
Frazier House, East Quay, Mevagissey. Tel: 01726 843568.
Open Easter–Sep, daily.
**Lost Gardens of Heligan**
Pentewan, near Mevagissey.
Tel: 01726 844157/843566.
Open all year daily except Christmas Day.

**Mevagissey Aquarium**
South Quay. Tel: 01726 843305.
Open Apr–Sep, daily.

**Mineral Tramways Discovery Centre**
Old Cowlin's Mill, Carn Brea,
Redruth. Tel: 01209 612917.
Open all year, most days. Free.

**Newquay Sea Life Centre**
Towan Promenade. Tel: 01637
872822. Open daily.

**Perranzabuloe Folk Museum**
Oddfellows Hall, Ponsmere
Road, Perranporth. Tel: 01872
573368. Open Easter and May
to mid-Oct most days.

**Polmassick Vineyard**
St Ewe, near Mevagissey.
Tel: 01726 842239. Open
Jun–Sep, most days.

**Probus Gardens**
Probus, near Truro. Tel: 01726
882597. Open all year daily.

**Royal Cornwall Museum**
River Street, Truro. Tel: 01872
272205. Open all year, closed
Sun and Bank Hol Mon.

**St Agnes Museum**
Penwinnick Road. Tel: 01872
552181. Open Apr–Sep daily.
Free.

**St Mawes Castle**
Tel: 01326 270526. Open all
year, most days.

**Trelissick Garden**
Feock, near Truro. Tel: 01872
862090. Open Mar–Oct daily.

**Trerice**
near Newquay. Tel: 01637
875404. Open Apr–Oct most
days.

**Trewithen**
Grampound Road, near Truro.
Tel: 01726 883647/883794.
Gardens open Mar–Sep, most
days; nursery all year, weekdays;
house Apr–Aug, limited
opening.

**Wheal Martyn China Clay Heritage Centre**
Carthew, St. Austell. Tel: 01726
850362. Open Apr–Oct daily.

### SPECIAL INTEREST FOR CHILDREN

The following places may be of
interest to visitors with children.
Unless otherwise stated there
will be an admission charge.

**Dairy Land Farm World**
Tresillian Barton, Summercourt,
near Newquay. Tel: 01872
510246. Farm animals, milking
parlour, nature trail, museum.
Open late Mar–Oct, daily.

**Holywell Bay Leisure Park**
near Newquay. Tel: 01637
830095. Adventure rides and
activities. Open Easter–Sep,
daily.

**Lappa Valley Steam Railway**
St Newlyn East, near Newquay.
Tel: 01872 510317. 15in-gauge
steam railway trip to historic
mining complex, leisure area,
boating lake, other attractions.

**Newquay Zoo**
Trenance Leisure Park,
Newquay. Tel: 01637 873342.
Lions, bears, camels etc. Open
Easter–Oct, daily.

**St Agnes Leisure Park**
St Agnes. Tel: 01872 552793.
Dinosaur exhibition, Fairyland,
miniature models, gardens.
Open Apr–Oct, daily.

**Trenance Leisure Park**
Newquay. Extensive sport and
leisure facilities, amusements.
Open Easter–Oct, daily.

**Tunnels Through Time**
Newquay. Tel: 01637 873379.
Life-size characters depict
Cornwall's past. Open
Easter–early Oct, most days.

**World in Miniature**
Goonhavern, near Truro. Tel:
01872 572828. Famous
landmarks in miniature,
Adventure Dome, gardens.
Open late Mar–Oct.

## Shopping

**Camborne**
Large covered and open-air
market at Pool. Saturdays and
Sundays.

**Newquay**
Covered market daily at Chester
Road. Main shopping areas: Cliff
Road, East Street, Bank Street
and Fore Street.

**Par**
Large covered market at
Stadium Park, off the A390.
Saturday and Sunday. Also
open-air stalls on Sundays.

**St Austell**
Open market in town centre,
Fridays and Saturdays.
Shopping precinct, Old Market
House.

**Truro**
Pannier Market, Lemon Quay,
Monday to Saturday.
Lemon Street Market, Monday
to Saturday.
Main shopping areas: Boscawen
Street and Pydar Street.

### LOCAL SPECIALITIES

**Crafts**
Cornwall Crafts Association,
Trelissick Gardens, near Truro.
Open Mar–Dec daily.
Mid Cornwall Galleries, St Blazey
Gate, near St Austell. Tel: 01726
812131.

**Sheepskin and Pottery**
Tescan Sheepskin and Fosters
Pottery, Pool Industrial Estate,
Pool, Redruth. Tel: 01209
214101.

**Wine**
Polmassick Vineyard, St Ewe, near
Mevagissey. Tel: 01726 842239.
Open Jun–Sep, daily.

## The Performing Arts

**Lane Theatre**
Newquay. Tel: 01637 876945.
Popular comedy season
May–Oct, midweek.

**St Austell Arts Centre**
87 Truro Road, St Austell.
Tel: 01726 73949.

## Sports, Activities and the Outdoors

### ANGLING

**Sea**
*Mevagissey:*
Mevagissey Shark & Angling
Centre. Tel: 01726 843430.
*Newquay:*
Moonraker Angling. Tel: 01637
871166

**Coarse**
Porth Reservoir, near Newquay.
Tel: 01837 871565.

### BEACHES

**Crinnis Beach: Carlyon Bay**
Long beach, very popular. Blue
Flag award.

**Crantock Beach**
Popular. Backed by sand dunes.
Estuary at north end dangerous
for swimming. Lifeguard.

**Holywell Bay**
Large sandy beach with dunes,
surfing, lifeguard.

**Mawgan Porth**
Popular family beach. Lifeguard.

**Newquay**
Watergate Bay: large west-facing beach. Can be breezy, lifeguard; Porth Beach: safe bathing, dogs not allowed; Lusty Glaze: pleasant beach backed by cliffs, lifeguard; Tolcarne Beach: large beach, surfing, lifeguard; Towan Beach: large sandy beach, lifeguard; Great Western: popular surfing beach; Fistral Beach: large, popular, west-facing, international surfing venue. Lifeguard.

**Pendower and Carne**
Pendower is popular; Carne is greatly reduced at highest tides. Voluntary dog ban at Carne.

**Perranporth**
Village beach: popular, use poop scoops. Lifeguard. Penhale Beach: very long, good for families and surfers.

**Porthtowan**
Large beach, popular. Lifeguard. Dogs not allowed.

**Portreath**
Popular north-facing beach, dogs not allowed.

**Roseland Peninsula**
Small beaches in St Mawes area and at Portscatho. Dogs not allowed May–Sep.

**St Agnes**
Trevaunance: quite small, popular, but greatly reduced during highest tides, surfing, lifeguard, dogs on leads; Chapel Porth: long stretch of sand, reduced greatly at high tide. Surfing, lifeguard.
Lifeguards, where indicated, are on summer service. Dogs are not allowed on several popular beaches from Easter to the end of September. Owners must use poop scoops in winter.

### BOAT TRIPS

**Mevagissey and Newquay**
Pleasure trips available from booking offices at harbours.

**Truro**
River Trips from Town Quay or Malpas (depending on tides) to Falmouth. Tel: 01326 374241/ 313234.

### BOWLING

There are bowling clubs at Newquay, Truro and Veryan. For information please contact the local Tourist Information Centre.

### COUNTRY PARKS AND NATURE RESERVES

**Tehidy Country Park**
Near Camborne. Tel: 01209 714494.

### CYCLING

A network of quiet lanes offers good cycling between the main roads and main centres of the area. Cycling is not permitted on footpaths or the coast path.

### CYCLE HIRE

**Newquay**
Cycle Revolution, 7 Beach Road. Tel: 01637 872634.

**Mevagissy**
Pentewan Valley Cycle Hire, 1 West End, Pentewan. Tel: 01726 844242.

### FLYING

Cornish Gliding and Flying Club. Trevellas Airfield, St Georges Hill, Perranporth. Tel: 01872 572124. Gliding: holiday courses.

### GOLF COURSES

**Camborne**
Tehidy Park Golf Club. Tel: 01209 842208.

**Newquay**
Holywell Bay Golf Club. Tel: 01637 830095. Newquay Golf Club, Tower Road, Newquay. Tel: 01637 874354. Treloy Golf Club. Tel: 01637 878554.

**St Austell**
Carlyon Bay Hotel and Golf Club, near St. Austell. Tel: 01726 814250. Porthpean Golf Club, Porthpean. Tel: 01726 64613. St Austell Golf Club, Tregongeeves. Tel: 01726 74756.

**Truro**
Killiow Golf Park, Killiow Kea. Tel: 01872 261055. Truro Golf Club, Treliske. Tel: 01872 78684.

### HORSE-RIDING

**Blackwater**
Chiverton Riding Centre, Silverwell. Tel: 01872 560471.

**Newquay**
Trenance Riding Stables. Tel: 01637 872699.

*Bustling Newquay offers holiday shopping*

**St Agnes**
Goonbell Riding Centre, Goonbell Farm. Tel: 01872 552063.

## Annual Events and Customs

Gig racing is now a major activity in Cornwall, many villages and towns have their own gigs. Newquay is a major centre, with regular events.

**Camborne**
Trevithick Day. Last Saturday in April. Street stalls, dancing, parade of steam engines.

**Charlestown**
Regatta Week. Late July.

**Mevagissey**
Mevagissey Feast Week. Last week June

**Newquay**
Cornwall Gardens Festival. April to May.
Hot-Air Balloon Festival early May.
Newquay 1900 Week. July.
Victorian Dress Festival, parade, torchlight procession, craft markets.
British National Surf Championships. July.
RAF St Mawgan International Air Day. Early August.
Pro-Am Surf Championships. August.
World Life Saving Champion-ships, Fistral Beach. August.
Championship Gig Racing. September.
Newquay Music and Flower Festival. September.

**St Mawes**
Town Regatta. August.

# The Lizard Peninsula: Falmouth and Helston

The Lizard Peninsula is a large area of flat downland fringed by dramatic sea cliffs of variegated serpentine and slate. The peninsula ends at Lizard Point, the most southerly point in Britain. Along its corrugated coastline lovely beaches line the edge of coves and bays. The Lizard is famous for the many rare plants that grow on its spacious heathland and on its coastal fringe. To the north of Lizard Point is the Helford River where a softer landscape of wooded creeks and quiet coastline leads on to the great natural harbour of Falmouth. The western gateway to the Lizard is the busy town of Helston and throughout the region there are quiet villages and hidden corners of great charm.

## SERPENTINE

The name serpentine describes perfectly the mottled and variegated rock for which the Lizard area is famous. The geological name is serpentinite, but it fails to slither off the tongue quite so smoothly. Serpentine is a dark rock that is either red or greyish-green in colour and is streaked with webbed veins of a lighter hue. It shines beautifully when it is polished and it has been used to make ornaments and furnishings since the early part of the 19th century. Serpentine is still cut and polished at small workshops on the Lizard. At Carleon Cove, a mile to the north of Cadgwith on the coast path, are the ruins of a large Serpentine works that employed over 100 people during the 19th century.

## CADGWITH   Map ref SW7214

Thatched and slate-roofed cottages crowd together at Cadgwith between encroaching hillsides and cliffs. A shingle beach runs to either side of a rocky promontory called the Todden. Beyond all this, sea and sky are full of light. Cadgwith is best visited on foot; there is a car park on the high ground above the village. Fishing boats still work from Cadgwith's beach where pilchards were once landed in vast quantities until the fishery declined early this century. Cadgwith's fishermen now use inkwell-shaped pots to catch lobster and crab, and gill nets to catch cod, pollack, monkfish and other species. The old buildings, known as cellers, where the pilchards were salted and pressed for oil, have been converted for modern use.

The small building on the cliff to the north of the cove was a coastguard watch house that was built over 100 years ago. A short walk along the coast path to the south of Cadgwith leads to the spectacular Devil's Frying-pan, a huge gulf in the vegetated cliffs where a sea cave collapsed centuries ago. (See Walk on page 78.)

The Lizard area is especially noted for the variety and value of its plant life. Pink thrift, the powder-blue squill, cliff bluebells and kidney vetch are prolific, but insignificant-looking plants may well be very rare and vulnerable. Visitors are asked not to pick even the most prolific wild flowers and to take care while walking.

## COVERACK   Map ref SW7818

Coverack is open to the sea, the village seeming to cling to the edge of its low cliffs and harbour walls. There is a through road, but it is allowed only grudging passage at the heart of Coverack by a steep and awkward corner. Pilchard fishing was the mainstay of Coverack from the medieval period until the early 20th century and the village still has a raw edge of the sea to it. The authentic atmosphere of the old village has managed to survive the impact of more modern development that has attached to it. And if you wonder why a Cornish fishing village should have a Paris Hotel, the establishment is named after a ship that was stranded off the coast of Coverack in 1899.

Just over 2 miles (3.2km) north of Coverack is St Keverne, a village full of character with a compact square and an impressive church. It served the dual purpose of spiritual and navigational guidance, as its ribbed spire was a landmark for local fishermen. This stretch of the coastline was treacherous to larger vessels, especially around the off-shore reef known as the Manacles, a vivid name made even more menacing by its derivation from the Cornish *Maen Eglos*, the Church Stones. On the inner walls of St Keverne's beautiful church, and within its churchyard, the memorials to drowned sailors make poignant but compelling reading that is worthy of a Conrad novel. It is impossible to visit here without considering the price of great maritime traditions, but there are a number of good pubs in the square to relieve the melancholy afterwards.

**GOURMET DELIGHTS**

Shellfish are a Cornish delight. Crab, lobster and crawfish are caught by fishermen who work from small coves such as those around the Lizard. The inkwell pots that they use were once made from willows or 'withies', but are now made of metal and synthetic materials. The exotic-looking red-gold crawfish are more often caught in tangle nets. In British waters they are mainly caught off Cornwall and can be mistaken for lobster by the undiscerning, even though they do not have the same huge claws – remember that lobsters are blue-black when caught, red when cooked. Lobster is delicious; crawfish is meatier and sweeter-fleshed; crab tastes like Cornwall. Try them all.

*In its splendidly isolated position on the coast, Coverack was once a smugglers' haven*

# Devil's Coast and Country Churches

*A coast walk from Cadgwith past the Devil's Frying-pan and on to Landewednack church in the lee of The Lizard. The return is along field paths and the tops of the broad walls, known as 'hedges' in Cornwall and past the isolated church of St Grada. Generally level with a few moderate inclines and awkward stiles. Can be very muddy after rain.*

Time: 2½ hours. Distance: 3 miles (4.8km).
Location: 10 miles (16.1km) south of Helston.
Start: Cadgwith car park. Situated at the top of the village,
1½ miles (2.4km) off the A3083 north of The Lizard.
(OS grid ref: SW719147).
OS Maps: Explorer 103 (The Lizard) 1:25,000
Landranger 203 (Land's End, The Lizard and Isles of Scilly),
204 (Truro and Falmouth) 1:50,000.
See Key to Walks on page 121.

## ROUTE DIRECTIONS

Leave the car park from its bottom corner, signed **'Cadgwith'**, and follow a footpath downhill between houses to the main village road. Turn right, then follow the road steeply uphill, first right, then left. Where the road bends sharply right, keep straight ahead, then cross a stile by the coast path sign and sign to Devil's Frying-pan. Follow a surfaced track and continue steeply, past houses, until you reach the end of an access road at Inglewidden.

Turn left, signed 'Devil's Frying-pan', pass in front of Townplace cottage and keep straight ahead across a small meadow, then follow the coast path above the spectacular **Devil's Frying-pan**. Continue for a mile (1.6km) above **Dollar Ogo, Chough's Ogo, Polgwidden and Parn Voose Cove**. Just beyond Parn Voose Cove pass a wooden navigation landmark, then continue down a winding path through old quarries to reach a lane at **Church Cove** (NT).

Turn right and follow the lane uphill to Landewednack church. Just before the church turn right through the small car park and follow a track round to the left, then right for 100 yards (91m), to a gate. Cross a stile into a field.

*At high tide sea-water hisses and bubbles into the Devil's Frying-pan*

Keep straight ahead along a faint path, then bear down left between gorse bushes. In a few yards go right through a bramble gap to a stream.

Carefully descend awkward slate steps, cross the stream, turn left, then left again along a muddy track. Follow the track uphill and round to the right, then go sharply left and uphill to cross a stile by a gate.

Turn right, keep by the edge of two fields, climb a stile on your right and turn left up a muddy farm track. At a concrete track, bear right in front of the large farmhouse at Trethvas, then head down a short track, signed 'Cadgwith'.

Clamber up slate steps onto a broad field hedge and follow the path along the top of the hedge through several fields. Soon descend from the hedge-path, cross a field to a stile by a gate and continue to a surfaced road. Turn left and just past Anvoaze, go right along a grassy track to the **Church of St Grada**.

Leave the churchyard by a stile in the far left-hand corner proceed down the field edge to a stile and enter a very large field. Keep ahead, keeping left of a telegraph pole, to reach a hidden stile in the bottom hedge and a road. To your left, behind the opposite hedge, is ancient St Ruan's Well.

Turn right along the road then just beyond a right-hand junction, go right between granite gate posts. Return to the car park, 300 yards (274m).

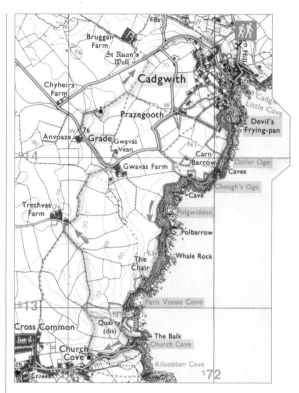

### POINTS OF INTEREST

**Cadgwith**
One of Cornwall's most picturesque fishing villages, Cadgwith is still a vigorous working community that wins a living from the sea.

**Devil's Frying-pan**
This remarkable feature is the result of the collapse of the roof of a massive sea cave. Its Cornish name is Hugga Dridgee. The 'frying pan' reference derives from the effect of the sea, hissing and bubbling through the arched exit far below.

**Dollar Ogo, Chough's Ogo, Polgwidden and Parn Voose Cove**
These cliff features along this stretch of coast are steep and dramatic. The term 'ogo' means cave in Cornish and is a common usage. Above Parn Voose Cove, the path leads past a navigation beacon called The Balk which is used in conjunction with another beacon at Bass Point to the west, to assist vessels to keep clear of the dangerous offshore reef Vrogue Rock.

**Church Cove**
A sheltered valley, exquisitely draped with flowers in spring and summer, leads inland from the coast to the attractive little church of Landewednack, the name of which derives from a Breton abbey whose abbot in the 6th century was descended from a Cornish family.

**The Church of St Grada**
This modest little building is in a striking position, raised above fields that are always wet during prolonged rain. It has been a sacred site for many centuries, and was named in medieval times as *Sancte Crucis*, the Holy Cross.

Not be missed are the various river and sea cruises available from Falmouth's Prince of Wales Pier and from other boarding points around the estuary. Ferries leave for Flushing and St Mawes, and when the tide allows, there are cruises upriver to Malpas from where a five-minute bus ride connects with Truro. An enjoyable trip can be made upriver to Tolverne on the Roseland Peninsula. If you are confident of having good sea legs, there are trips along the coast and then up the Helford River; evening cruises on the Fal are another option along with sea-angling trips from the Prince of Wales Pier.

*Pendennis Castle, dating back to the 16th century, was besieged by Cromwell's troops in the Civil War*

## FALMOUTH  Map ref SW8032

Vessels of all types and sizes still bustle in and out of Falmouth, lending excitement and atmosphere to one of the world's largest natural harbours. Falmouth developed as a port after Henry VIII built Pendennis and St Mawes castles, the guardians of the Fal Estuary. Both are built in the distinctive clover-leaf design and St Mawes is particularly renowned as a fine example of military architecture. Visitors here can explore the dungeons, barrack rooms and cannon-lined castle walls.

During the late 17th century the port became a packet station, from where small, fast-sailing brigantines took mail to north-west Spain, and in later years to North America, the West Indies and South America. Gold and silver bullion was carried and the packets provided a passenger service. By the 1830s over 40 packets worked out of Falmouth. They were well-armed against privateers, French naval hostility and even Algerian pirates. The crews supplemented their meagre wages with smuggling and by carrying unofficial goods; there are rich tales of villainy and swashbuckling. The packet service had transferred to Southampton by 1850 but Falmouth's position as a major port was secured by a vigorous pilchard fishery, the development of Falmouth docks and a thriving shipbuilding industry. Ship repair, bunkering, cargo handling and yacht building are industries which continue today.

Falmouth's rather straggling form gives it less unity than might be expected of a port, as the town follows the riverside through a chain of linking main streets, but this makes it intriguing to explore. It is centred on The Moor, once a muddy creek and now emphatically urban, and it is here that you will find the Falmouth Art Gallery, well worth a visit, on the upper floor of the old Passmore Edwards Free Library. As well as changing

exhibitions there are permanent displays of paintings including those of Henry Scott Tuke, the Victorian painter who spent his last years near Falmouth.

From the Moor, Webber Street leads to the Prince of Wales Pier. Market Street is the first of Falmouth's long chain of streets that leads along the riverfront. Part way down is Bell's Court where the Maritime Museum outlines Cornwall's and Falmouth's powerful maritime history. The walk along Market Street, Church Street, and Arwenack Street should be varied by diversions to the town quays from where there are panoramic views across the rivermouth. The old harbour tug, *St Denys*, moored at Custom House Quay, is part of the Maritime Museum.

Some of Falmouth's many engaging features include the 111-step Jacob's Ladder that leads up from the Moor, and watch for the recurring theme of Falmouth's 'Opes', the narrow passageways that run between the town's buildings.

But the great estuary of the River Fal is the overriding attraction. The various piers that project into the river seem to draw the town seaward. Pendennis Castle lies on the headland to the east of Falmouth and is easily reached from the waterfront. Of the several pleasant beaches along Falmouth's southern seafront, Gyllyngvase is the largest and most popular. North-west of Falmouth, at the tidal head of the Penryn River, is Penryn, more ancient as a port than its sprawling neighbour. Old Penryn has some fine Tudor and Jacobean architecture as well as later Georgian features.

*Falmouth docks were second only to London in the heyday of sail, and are still busy today*

**RUM-AND-SHRUB**

Old Cornwall had its own black economy during the 18th and 19th centuries in the form of smuggling. This illicit trade created the famous Cornish drink of rum-and-shrub, in which rum is sweetened by the addition of an alcoholic cordial made from spices and herbs. This was done because barrels of smuggled rum that had been left hidden in sea-washed caves, or even submerged to await collection, sometimes became tainted with sea water. Cornish fishermen and miners believed rum-and-shrub helped cure chest colds. No such excuse is needed on holiday.

*The rocks at Gunwalloe have witnessed many a shipwreck*

**LIZARD LAKES**

Cornwall has few natural lakes of any size but there are several reservoirs that make a pleasant change from the sea. The Argal and College Waterpark is only about 2 miles (3.2km) from Falmouth along the A394. The linked reservoirs are tree-fringed and very peaceful, with much bird-life and pleasant paths skirting the shorelines. Coarse fishing is available all year and the fly-fishing season is from March to October. Stithians Lake is within easy reach of Falmouth and Helston along the A394. There is a car park on the east side of the lake near the dam and another at its north end, near the water sports centre.

## GUNWALLOE  Map ref SW6522

The road to Gunwalloe ends at Church Cove where an intriguing little church nestles close to the edge of eroded cliffs. The cliffs have been stabilised by the introduction of huge rocks to create a breakwater. North of the church is the noisily-named Jangye-ryn Cove. Inland lie extensive sand dunes; a golf course crowns the green swell of the higher land in rather odd counterpoint.

The coastline is often lively, as it is west-facing and open to boisterous seas. Shipwrecks were common during the days of sail when vessels became trapped within the horns of Mount's Bay; the price of not giving the Lizard a wide berth was grief on Gunwalloe's shoreline. The name of Dollar Cove below the church reflects the loss of a Spanish treasure ship in the 1780s.

Halzephron Cove and Gunwalloe Fishing Cove lie just north of Church Cove and can be reached along the coast path. The National Trust has solved the problem of scattered parking at Gunwalloe with a screened car park on the approach to Church Cove. (The Walk on page 92 just touches on Gunwalloe.) The problem of sea erosion is another matter. The sea is threatening to break through the neck of land between Dollar Cove and Church Cove and large blocks of granite have been tipped onto the beach to break the force of the waves.

## HELFORD   Map ref SW7526

There is irresistible romance attached to Helford and its tree-shrouded river and creeks. The price is that the area can become uncomfortably busy during popular holiday periods. But the dense nature of this serene landscape rewards those who explore further than Helford itself, lovely though the village is. The countryside is passive, compared with the extremes of the coast, and though access along the riverbank is limited in places, there are a number of fine walks to be enjoyed from Helford.

Just to the west lies the famous Frenchman's Creek, romanticised by both Sir Arthur Quiller-Couch and Daphne du Maurier and still enchanting today, even when the falling tide reveals an expanse of mud. A path leads east from Helford to the coast at Dennis Head and to St Anthony and Gillan. These quiet places are best visited on foot; parking is difficult and is not encouraged.

A seasonal passenger ferry from Helford sails to Helford Passage on the north bank, from where the National Trust's Glendurgan Garden and the adjacent Trebah Garden can be visited. Glendurgan is one of the great sub-tropical gardens of the South West, situated on the banks of the Helford River near Mawnan Smith. Rhododendrons, camellias and hydrangeas flourish amidst lovely woodland and there is an engaging maze. Trebah Garden has a fine water garden among its attractions. The smaller garden at Penjerrick, just over a mile north of Mawnan Smith, is where Chilean firebushes, magnolias and azaleas flourish.

### BIKING ROUND THE BACKROADS

The maze of narrow lanes south of the Helford River make enjoyable cycling routes, which are best tackled during the quieter periods. Good map-reading and navigation is part of the challenge. A pleasant route starts from Helston and follows the lanes to Gweek from the A394, then follows the south bank of the Helford via Constantine Quay and Mawgan Cross, passing St Mawgan Church, and then continuing across the head of Mawgan Creek to eventually reach St Martin. From here, go north, then east above Manaccan and Helford to reach St Anthony. Return west alongside Gillan Creek, then go south to reach Newtown-in-St Martin. Turn left here to reach the B3293. Turn right for the A3083 for Helston and perhaps visit Trelowarren on the way.

*The tranquil waters at Helford hide a legendary sea-monster, Morgawr, first glimpsed in 1926*

# Helford River and The Lizard

*An absorbing 62-mile (99km) drive past some lovely lakes and on through the Helford River area to The Lizard, Britain's most southerly point. The south side of the Helford Estuary is a delightful landscape of wood-fringed creeks and inlets. Helford is worth a diversion from the main route of the tour, although access is down narrow lanes and driving can become restricted during busy holiday periods.*

## ROUTE DIRECTIONS

See Key to Car Tours on page 120.
Leave Helston on the B3297, signed 'Redruth'. After 6 miles (9.6km) reach Nine Maidens and turn right onto an unclassified road, signed 'Carnmenellis'. After 1¼ miles (2km), at a T-junction at Penmarth, turn left, signed 'Stithians'. Continue, with Stithians Reservoir on the right. The reservoir is noted as a water sports centre and for its birdlife. Pass the Golden Lion Inn and continue across a causeway. At the next junction turn right, signed 'Stithians', and continue through Tresevern and Goonlaze. (Note: access road to Stithians dam and car park, just after Goonlaze). Continue through Stithians (toilets), then, on the other side of the village, at a crossroads, go

*Looking across the river from Helford's sailing club*

straight across and down Tregonning Road, signed 'Mabe'. Follow a narrow lane for 1¼ miles (2km) then go right at a T-junction, signed 'Longdowns'. In three quarters of a mile (1.2km), just after a quarry, go left at a T-junction. Soon, reach the A394 and turn left, signed 'Falmouth'. A short distance ahead, and just past a garage, branch right, signed 'Mabe'. Reach Mabe Burnthouse and, at a crossroads at the centre of the village, turn right, signed 'Mawnan' and 'Constantine'. Keep left at the next junction, signed 'Mawnan Smith'. A short distance further on, a side road branches right to **Argal and College Water Park** (toilets). There is a car-parking area and there are lovely waterside walks.

On the main route, follow signs for Mawnan Smith. Go directly over a crossroads and continue for 2 miles (3.2km) to reach Mawnan Smith, a

pleasant village within lovely surroundings. Keep right by the Red Lion Inn, signed 'Budock Vean', and follow signs for Helford Passage and Constantine. Continue, passing **Glendurgan Garden**, a woodland valley garden of 40 acres, then pass the equally fine, 25-acre **Trebah Gardens**. Follow signs for Porth Navas and Constantine along a winding and often narrow lane (with passing places). Pass through Porth Navas and follow signs for Constantine.

At a T-junction, go left through Constantine. On the far side of the village ignore the first left turn signed 'Vicarage Lane, Gweek' and take the next left turn signed 'Gweek'. Pass through Brill and turn left at the next junction signed 'Gweek'. Go through Gweek, then go left by a thatched house, signed 'Mawgan' and 'St Keverne'.

Continue through a wooded area and, at a roundabout, go left, signed 'Mawgan'. Drive carefully through Mawgan, pass Mawgan church and then follow signs for Manaccan and Helford along a narrow and winding road with some steep inclines and sharp bends. Pass through St Martin and reach Newtown-in-St Martin. Go straight through the village. On the far side reach a junction with a road leading left signed 'Manaccan, Helford'. (Divert left here if you wish to visit the village of Helford.) On the main route keep ahead, pass through Tregidden, turn left at a T-junction, then continue through Tregowris. Follow the signs for St Keverne through several junctions to reach St Keverne (toilets).

From St Keverne square follow the B3293, signed 'Coverack' and 'Helston'. In

2½ miles (4km) turn left, signed 'Kennack Sands' and 'Cadgwith'. (A mile further along the B3293 is the **Goonhilly Satellite Earth Station**, a complex of giant communication antennas with an excellent Visitors' Centre.)

On the main route, drive down an arrow-straight road to reach Kuggar. At a junction, turn right signed 'Cadgwith'. At the next crossroads go forward, signed 'St Ruan and Cadgwith, Alternative Route For Heavy Vehicles'. Continue through St Ruan and after about half a mile (0.8km) pass a side road leading left. (300 yards down

this side road is large car park for Cadgwith.) On the main route keep ahead, and continue following signs for The Lizard. At a junction with the A3083, turn left for Lizard Point (toilets). Return along the A3083 to Helston, passing Culdrose Naval Air Station on the way.

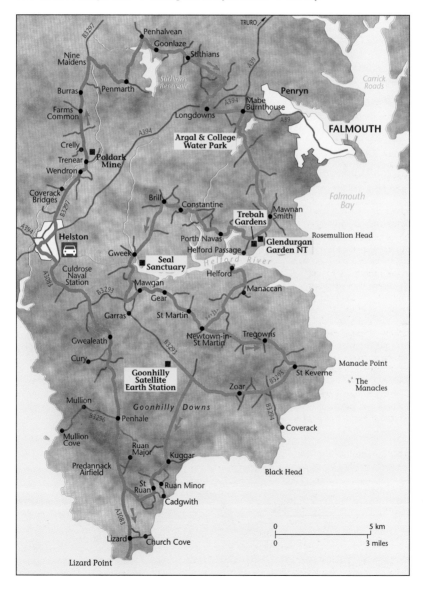

# Romantic Helford River and Rosemullion Head

A peaceful year-round walk round Rosemullion Head and along the north of the Helford River, with a visit to an ancient Cornish church on the way. There are a few short inclines and woodland paths may be muddy.

Time: 3 hours. Distance: 4½ miles (7.2km).
Location: 4½ miles (7.2km) south of Falmouth.
Start: National Trust car park above Durgan, ½ mile (0.8km).
south of Mawnan Smith. (OS grid ref: SW775277).
OS Maps: Explorer 103 (The Lizard) 1:25,000
Landranger 204 (Truro and Falmouth) 1:50,000.
See Key to Walks on page 121.

### ROUTE DIRECTIONS

Turn left out of the car park, following the road for about a quarter of a mile (0.4km), then take the arrowed path on the right to a slate stile (slippery when wet). Follow field edges, then proceed along an enclosed path behind houses keeping ahead, over a stone stile at a junction with a path from the left. Where this path ends cross a stile, keep to the field edge to a further stile and continue along a wide track, past houses, to reach the road at **Mawnan Smith**.

Turn right, pass a junction with Old Church Road, then, in 200 yards (183m), turn right down a surfaced lane, go through a gate (signposted) and follow a track down through trees to join the coast path. Turn right and descend to a small beach by a slipway.

Follow the coast path crossing a small stream. Go over a stile and follow the field edge, then follow a path up the open field to a stile

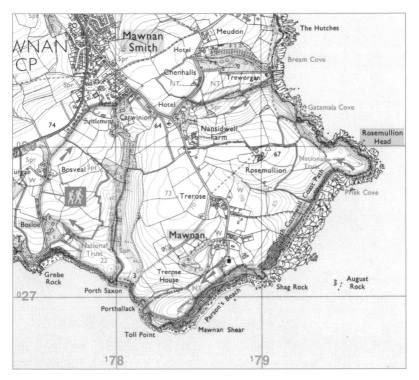

into a small wood. Leave the wood by a stile then continue uphill across a field to a gate and a National Trust sign indicating **Rosemullion Head**.

Bear left downhill on the coast path, to round the headland, then continue along the bottom edge of fields to a stile. Continue through fields to reach Mawnan Glebe (NT). Climb a stile into woods, then soon descend a flight of wooden steps. After 150 yards (137m), take the path on the right by a small holly bush. Go uphill to some stone steps, then bear right inland to **Mawnan Church**.

Return to the coast path and turn right. Leave the woods by a stile and follow the coast path eventually rounding Toll Point on the northern shores of the **Helford River** to reach Porthallack and then Porth Saxon. Cross in front of the boathouse here and keep to the coast path along the bottom edge of an open field to a stone stile, then turn immediately right, signed 'Garden Walk to Durgan Crossroads'. Proceed uphill alongside the hedge to reach a cross-path. Keep straight on through a small plantation of mainly young oaks and follow the wide path left, through the grounds of **Bosloe House**. At the top of some stone steps, keep right and climb more steps. Continue to a gate (Candy's Gate) on to the lane by Bosloe gatehouse. Cross over and turn right along a path parallel with the lane back to the car park.

### POINTS OF INTEREST

**Mawnan Smith**
The name of this pleasant, village relates to the nearby church, Smith being a Saxon addition relating to a blacksmith's shop that was probably the early focus of this rich farming country.

**Rosemullion Head**
A modest headland in Cornish terms, Rosemullion would have been suited to an Iron-Age promontory enclosure but there is no positive evidence of this and traces of earthworks amidst the summit scrub are of old shooting butts. The Head supports a wealth of wild flowers, such as the cliff bluebell in spring, and the early purple orchid. Pink thrift, white sea campion, birdsfoot trefoil and many other plants also grow here.

**Mawnan Church**
Mawnan church probably originated in the 6th century as a small stone cell or simple enclosure founded by a Breton, or Irish missionary. Pre-Christian remnants of a surrounding earthwork remain, but were damaged in the early 20th century when the churchyard was enlarged.

**The Helford River**
This picturesque river with its pattern of tidal creeks is a legacy of changes of sea-level millions of years ago. Falling sea levels caused over-deepening of the river valleys, and when levels rose again, the sea flooded the valleys. The effect of tides creates the two faces of the Helford River, mud-pack and mirrored calm.

**Bosloe**
This elegant country residence with its ornamental gardens was built in the early 1880s. The house and 150 acres of riverside land was bought by the National Trust in 1980 and is now part of their holiday accommodation.

*The Helford River is closely hemmed in by trees*

### HELSTON FURRY DANCE

On or about 8 May each year Helston stages its famous Furry Dance, a name derived from the Cornish *fer*, meaning feast or fair, and harking back to pre-Christian celebrations of spring. It is known also as Helston Flora. The modern event is colourful but decorous, compared with Victorian reports of its having been a 'barbarous carnival', with processional dances through the streets, and in and out of selected houses and shops. Men wear morning coats and top hats, woman wear long, brightly coloured dresses and the Helston equivalent of Easter bonnets. The repetitive tune played by Helston band is subdued but compulsive. Mummers act out the legend of St Michael slaying a dragon through the early morning streets. Helston is swamped with people on the day, but the experience is quite unforgettable.

*Helston's Guildhall, decorated for the famous Furry Dance celebrations*

### HELSTON   Map ref SW6527

Helston is the true gateway to the Lizard. It was a port until the silting of the River Cober landlocked the town, but historically its main importance was as the trading centre of the area and as a Coinage town (see page 26). It thrived throughout the medieval period and for several centuries thereafter despite fluctuations in metal mining. The name of Coinagehall Street is witness to the town's history and its generous width reflects its market history; the town is still a very good shopping centre. There is a grand view down Coinagehall Street to the Gothic-style gateway of the bowling green and to the green fields rising beyond. The handsome Guildhall dominates the top of the street and the nearby Victorian Market House is quite stylish for its time.

There is a good museum in the Market House. Church Street runs down to the left of the Market House and then up to the Church of St Michael, which is 18th century and rather dull. Church Street and the adjoining Cross Street have good Georgian façades and there is a strong period atmosphere in this part of the town. Helston is justly famous for its annual Furry, or Flora Dance. Proximity to the splendid Penrose estate and Loe Bar adds to Helston's attractions. (See Walk on page 92.) Penrose can be reached from the Coronation Gardens and Boating Lake at the bottom end of the town.

Off the B3293 St Keverne road, about 3½ miles (5.6km) from Helston, is Trelowarren House. It has been the home of the Vyvyan family since the early 15th century and the east wing dates from that time. The attached chapel has an attractive rococo-Gothic interior, and there are craft workshops, an art gallery and a restaurant. Within the estate is Halligue Fogou, a good example of an Iron-Age underground chamber, the purpose of which is uncertain.

## KYNANCE COVE  Map ref SW6612

Victorian 'excursionists' first visited Kynance with their painting kits and sketch books and the cove was visited by a poet, Tennyson, and a prince, Albert. Kynance satisfied perfectly the romantic ideal of the picturesque in Nature. The whole of the beach is awash at high tide and emerges fresh and shining as each day dawns. The gnarled monoliths of serpentine that rise at intervals from the beach create a beautiful seascape. The largest is Asparagus Island, with Steeple Rock and the Sugar Loaf lying between it and the mainland. Part of the charm of Kynance lies in its unexpectedness, hidden as it is below the edge of the sometimes unnerving flatness of the Lizard Peninsula.

The cove and the cliffland to the east are in the care of the National Trust, which has provided a car park above Kynance and a viewpoint for disabled visitors. Descent to the Cove is steep, and the return is quite strenuous. Care should be taken if swimming off the cove – the tide comes in rapidly and the currents close to shore are dangerous.

The Kynance area is of great biological importance. Rare species grow in the area including sedges and tiny liverworts. Spiders, moths and even a rare European woodlouse are also found here. The mild climate, and a maritime environment partly explain the richness of local wildlife. The most striking symbol of the whole Lizard area is the Cornish Heath, a type of heather with lilac and white flowers, common in the Lizard area, but very rare elsewhere in Britain.

*At low tide look for delicate colours in the serpentine of Kynance Cove*

### SEAHAWKS...

Just outside Helston is the Royal Naval Air Station Culdrose, the largest helicopter base in Europe. Culdrose has contributed greatly to the economy and life of the area, it's Air-Sea Rescue squadron is famous for the daring rescues of civilians on land and sea using Sea King helicopters. There is a public viewing area on the road to Gweek.

### ...AND SEALS

Gweek, just beyond Culdrose, is the home of the famous Seal Sanctuary, Europe's largest rescue centre for seals. Up to 30 injured seal pups a year are cared for at the hospital and returned to the sea when they are fit and healthy. Those that are too badly disabled are given a new home at the sanctuary.

The Lizard Downs are rich in ancient artefacts that date from a time when early man found reasonable grazing on the poorly drained soil. The 20th century has contributed its own artefacts. Sprouting from the unrelentingly flat landscape at Goonhilly are British Telecom's satellite dish aerials. They are futuristic and fascinating. Further inland, the lazily revolving tower vanes of a wind farm increase the surrealism. Goonhilly's dishes play a celestial game of ping-pong, bouncing signals off orbiting satellites. The complex, known as the Goonhilly Satellite Earth Station, has a well-organised visitor centre and guided tours.

*The cliffs at Lizard Point tower up to 180 feet above sea level*

## LIZARD DOWNS   Map ref SW7521

The serpentine soil of the Lizard supports a remarkable variety of rare plants, many of them of southern European origin. The Lizard's mild climate encourages these plants but the main reason for the area's botanical uniqueness is that the Lizard was joined to the European land mass thousands of years ago, when these plants spread this far north and flourished on what are now the peninsula's coastal fringes. The plants remained when sea levels rose during the post-glacial period and Britain became an island.

There are subtle distinctions between species and a specialist's knowledge is required to identify many of the plants. But everyone can recognise and enjoy the attractive Cornish Heath, *Erica Vagans*, a type of heather found in substantial quantities only on the the Lizard. It has dark green leaves and spikes of small pink or lilac flowers. Closer to the cliff tops, the blue spring squill, the pink thrift and the creamy sea campion contribute to an exquisite mosaic of wild flowers in spring and summer.

## LIZARD POINT   Map ref SW6912

Lizard village is rather open and fragmented, but is a convenient base to explore Lizard Point, the most southerly point in Britain, and its adjoining coastline. You can park at the Point, where there is an old lifeboat station that has long been superseded by the modern station at Kilcobben Cove to the north-east. The view to seaward is exhilarating and the air can be mild even in midwinter, but when the tide is out, swathes of pungent seaweed may dull the edge of the bracing sea air.

The coast path leads west above high cliffs. To the east it passes through a green, sheltered landscape above cliffs draped with the invasive Hottentot Fig, or *mesembryanthemum,* originally a garden escapee now so prolific that it restricts other plant life. The Lizard's position jutting out into the Channel approaches, has made it dangerous to vessels. For a mile to seaward off Lizard Point the sea tumbles in frightening overfalls during stormy weather. To the north-east lies the blunt promontory of Black Head and beyond here the deadly Manacles Reef.

The fortress-like Lizard Lighthouse dominates the coast to the east. A warning light was first established here in 1612 but it had mixed success. Today's light is extremely powerful; it flashes every three seconds and can be seen in clear weather from up to 29 miles (46.7km) away. The fog signal is delivered by siren at 60 second intervals. You will notice it...

About 1½ miles (2.4km) east of Lizard Point is Church Cove at the mellow-sounding parish of Landewednack (See Walk on page 78). Landewednack's Church of St Wynwallow has a low tower of serpentine. It is named after a 6th-century Abbot of Landévennec in Brittany who is patron of a number of west Cornwall churches. The cove is reached on foot from the car park past thatched cottages and a serpentine workshop. A short walk south along the coast path leads to the remarkable cliffside site of the Lizard-Cadgwith lifeboat house. The outstanding record of the lifeboat echoes that of all Cornish lifeboats.

*Lizard's present lighthouse was built in 1751. Its beam is visible for many miles*

**RADIO WAVES**
The Lizard Peninsula has a famous association with Guglielmo Marconi, the Italian physicist who revolutionised communications through his development of wireless telegraphy. A memorial to Marconi stands on Angrouse Cliffs just south of Poldhu Cove near Mullion. It is easily reached along the coast path from either Mullion Cove or Poldhu Cove. From this point the first wireless message was transmitted across the Atlantic on 12 December, 1901, when the simple signal of a triple 's' was received by Marconi in Newfoundland. British Telecom's Earth Satellite Tracking Station on Goonhilly Downs has a pleasing continuity with Marconi's first flickering signals from Angrouse Cliffs.

# Cornish Waterland – The Loe

*A waterside walk round the beautiful lake known as The Loe, or Loe Pool, with an extension along the coast path to the south east. The woods are full of daffodils and bluebells in the spring. Some inclines on the coast, otherwise easy walking. Paths can be muddy on the east side of The Loe.*

Time: 3½ hours. Distance: 7 miles (11.2km)
Location: 1½ miles (2.4km) south-east of Helston.
Start: Car park at the top of Penrose Hill, located 100 yards (91m) down a side road, signed 'Loe Bar', going left off the B3304 between Helston and Porthleven.
(OS grid ref: SW639258).
OS Maps: Explorer 103 (The Lizard) 1:25,000
Landranger 203 (Land's End, The Lizard and Isles of Scilly) 1:50,000.
See Key to Walks on page 121.

## ROUTE DIRECTIONS

Take the path at the bottom end of the car park, cross a road, then descend wooden steps. Cross a driveway, turn right immediately along a second driveway, then keep left at a junction and cross an ornamental bridge. At the next junction, turn right, signed 'Loe Bar', and follow

*Sand and shingle form the natural barrier of Loe Bar, separating lake from sea*

the drive left in front of outbuildings near Penrose House.

Continue for just over a mile (1.6km) to reach a small lodge above Loe Bar. Pass through the lodge gate, turn sharp left round the end of a short wall and descend to **Loe Bar**. Note: entering the sea from Loe Bar is dangerous.

Cross Loe Bar parallel to the sea, then follow the grassy coast path uphill past the Anson **Monument**. After a

quarter of a mile (0.4km) keep right at a fork of paths along the cliff edge, then in a further half mile (0.8km), pass a sign for The Loe Pool. In a few yards, branch right along the cliff edge, then after 300 yards (273m), turn left by a wooden barrier and follow a path to reach a surfaced lane.

Turn right then on reaching a road junction, turn left along a narrow lane and after 100 yards (91m), climb a steep stile on your left into a field. Traverse the field towards a point midway between two gapways to a stile, then keep ahead across the following field and go over a stile. Walk beside the field hedge, turn right through a gate and follow a grassy track left to reach **Chyvarloe**.

Turn left on reaching a road, turn left, signed 'car park' and follow the rough track down to Loe Bar. Just before the track peters out, bear right, by NT sign Loe Bar, on to a narrow path, which soon merges with a sandy track curving round to the right. Follow the path along the edge of **The Loe**, round Carminowe Creek and on to Lower Pentire, then continue along a wide track for 200 yards (182m), before branching left onto a path. Go through a gate, keep to the poolside path and soon enter Degibna Wood. Keep left at a fork in the path, then bear left again at a junction. Go left where the path forks, then keep alongside the water's edge. At the edge of the wood go through a wooden fence, then keep by the water to reach a stile and gate. Cross a stream, go left along a track, then cross a field to reach Lower Nansloe.

Turn left along a track then, just before the chimney stack of the old Castle Wary Mine,

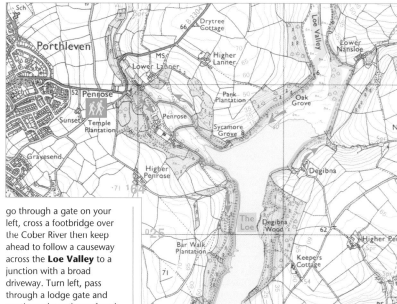

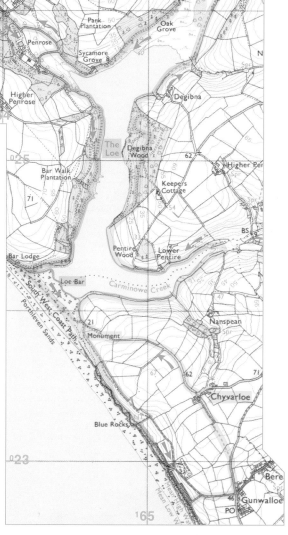

go through a gate on your left, cross a footbridge over the Cober River then keep ahead to follow a causeway across the **Loe Valley** to a junction with a broad driveway. Turn left, pass through a lodge gate and continue along the surfaced driveway to reach the Loe Bar signpost passed on the outward route. Keep ahead to return to the car park.

### POINTS OF INTEREST

**The Loe**
This stretch of water is the largest natural lake in Cornwall, though it lies within a wave's distance of the sea. Its name derives from the Cornish *logh*, meaning pool.

**Monument**
This rather obtrusive white cross commemorates the notorious wreck of the frigate *Anson* in 1807, when over 100 sailors were drowned. The inability of onlookers to mount a rescue motivated Helston man Henry Trengrouse, to develop the successful rocket apparatus for life saving.

**Chyvarloe**
A lovely example of a typically Cornish farm settlement. Much of the medieval character of the buildings and surrounding fields is still intact, thanks to imaginative restoration work by the National Trust.

**Loe Valley**
This is the valley of the River Cober, which runs into The Loe through Loe Marsh, a large area of reedbeds, willow and alder trees built up on silt washed down from numerous 19th-century mines. Castle Wary Mine was an 18th-century silver and lead mine.

### MULLION   Map ref SW6719

Mullion is a large village a short distance inland from the
harbour at Mullion Cove. There is a nice sense of
anticipation on first approaching Mullion and the village
lives up to expectations – a bustling place with an
excellent variety of shops, art and craft galleries and
good pubs. The Church of St Melanus has a remarkable
collection of bench-ends depicting lively characters,
jester as well as monk. Mullion Cove is fascinating. Big
cliffs and sea stacks, gold-leafed with yellow lichen,
enclose the narrow inlet and its substantial piers.
Offshore lies the bulky mass of Mullion Island, flickering
with seabirds.

The coast to the south is pleasantly remote, especially
around Predannack Head and Vellan Head, with
delightful coast walks to either side of the cove. Just to
the north is Polurrian Cove where there is a small beach
and further north again is Poldhu Cove with a good
sandy beach.

### PORTHLEVEN   Map ref SW6225

Porthleven was noted for its shipbuilding and fishing.
Both industries survive and today the village remains as
a fascinating, and truly Cornish, place. The centrepiece
inner harbour is lined along its quays with a mix of
shops, galleries, pubs, restaurants and cafés. On the
north side of the outer harbour is a wave-cut platform of
deeply pocketed and riven slate where a huge boulder,
the Giant's Rock, is exposed at low tide. It is believed to
be a glacial 'erratic' carried here embedded probably in
an ice floe during the last Ice Age.

Victorian villas on the South Quay create a pleasing
background to the harbour road and bustling quayside.
To the south-east, a road lined with colourful cottages
leads along the breezy cliff edge. Its continuation, Loe
Bar Road, leads to a car park, for the short walk to Loe
Bar and the Penrose estate (National Trust). (See Walk on
page 92). Swimming in this area is dangerous.

*Mullion harbour, or Porth
Mellin, is in the care of the
National Trust*

# The Lizard Peninsula: Falmouth and Helston

Leisure Information
Places of Interest
Shopping
The Performing Arts
Sports, Activities and the Outdoors
Annual Events and Customs

Checklist ✓

## Leisure Information

### TOURIST INFORMATION CENTRES

**Falmouth**
28 Killigrew Street. Tel: 01209 611102 and 01326 312300.
**Helston**
79 Meneage Street. Tel: 01326 565431.

### OTHER INFORMATION

**Coastguard**
Dial 999 and ask for the Coastguard Service.
**Cornwall Wildlife Trust**
Five Acres, Allet, Truro Tel: 01872 73939.
**English Heritage**
23 Savile Row, London. Tel: 0171 973 3434.
**Health**
Information on health problems is available Tel: 0800 665544. Dental Helpline Tel: 0800 371192.
**Environment Agency**
Manley House, Kestrel Way, Exeter. Tel: 01392 444000.
**National Trust in Cornwall**
Lanhydrock, Bodmin. Tel: 01208 74281.
**Parking**
Weekly parking tickets are available for car parks throughout the Lizard area. Apply in advance to Kerrier Council, or enquire at Helston Tourist Information Centre.
**South West Water**
Highercombe Park, Lewdown, Okehampton. For enquiries on recreation/fishing Tel: 01837 871565.
**Surf Call**
Report on local surfing conditions. Tel: 0891 333080.
**Weather Call**
South-west weather details. Tel: 0891 500758.

### ORDNANCE SURVEY MAPS

Explorer 1:25,000 Sheets 102, 103, 105
Landranger 1:50,000 Sheets 203, 204.

## Places of Interest

There will be an admission charge at the following places of interest unless otherwise stated.
**Cornwall Maritime Museum**
Bell's Court, Market Street, Falmouth. Tel: 01326 319963. Open all year, most days.
**Falmouth Art Gallery**
Municipal Buildings, The Moor. Tel: 01326 313863. Open all year most days. Free.
**Glendurgan Garden**
Mawnan Smith, near Falmouth. Tel: 01326 250906. Open Mar–Oct, most days.
**Godolphin House**
Godolphin Cross, Breage. Tel: 01736 762409. Mainly 16th-century house. Open during season on certain days.
**Goonhilly Satellite Earth Station**
Tel: 0800 679593. Open Apr–Nov, daily.
**Helston Folk Museum**
Old Butter Market, Church Street. Tel: 01326 564027. Open all year, most days. Free.
**National Seal Sanctuary**
Gweek. Tel: 01326 221874. Open all year, daily, except Christmas.
**Pendennis Castle**
Falmouth. Tel: 01326 316594. Open all year daily, except Christmas and New Year's Day.
**Poldark Mine and Heritage Complex**
Wendron, near Helston. Tel: 01326 573173. Underground mine tours, 18th-century village, displays, gardens, amusements, children's playground. Open Easter–Oct, daily.
**Trebah Gardens**
Mawnan Smith, near Falmouth.

Tel: 01326 250448. Open all year daily.

**Trelowarren**
Mawgan, Helston. Tel: 01326 221224. Woodland walks, gardens, galleries, pottery, countryside centre, restaurant. Open all year, daily.

### SPECIAL INTEREST FOR CHILDREN

The following places may be of interest to visitors with children. Unless otherwise stated there will be an admission charge.

**Flambards Village Theme Park**
Helston. Tel: 01326 573404. Flambards Victorian Village, Britain in the Blitz, Aeropark, fun rides. Open Easter–Oct, daily.

## Shopping

**Falmouth**
Best shopping area in High Street, Market Street and Church Street.

**Helston**
Street market Coinagehall Street, Monday and Saturday.

### LOCAL SPECIALITIES

**Crafts**
Beside The Wave, 10 Arwenack St, Falmouth. Trelowarren Gallery, near Helston. Open Easter to Christmas, most days.

**Pottery**
Trelowarren Pottery, near Helston. Tel: 01326 221583. Open all year daily.

**Wine**
Porthallow Vineyard, St Keverne. Wines, ciders, liqueurs. Tel: 01326 280050.

## The Performing Arts

**Falmouth Arts Centre**
Church Street, Falmouth. Tel: 01326 314566.

**Princess Pavilion**
Melvill Road, Falmouth. Tel: 01326 211222.

## Sports, Activities and the Outdoors

### ANGLING

**Sea**
Trips from Falmouth, Mullion

and Cadgwith.

**Coarse**
College Reservoir, Penryn, Falmouth. Tel: 01837 871565.

### BEACHES

**Falmouth**
Swanpool: dogs not allowed; Gyllngvase: large, popular, family beach, safe bathing, dogs not allowed.

**Gunwalloe**
Lifeguard at weekends, dogs not allowed.

**Kennack Sands**
Large beach, good area of sand, dogs not allowed.

**Kynance Cove**
Beach awash at high tide, popular, dogs not allowed.

**Maenporth**
South of Falmouth. Dogs not allowed.

**Poldhu**
Near Mullion. Popular beach, lifeguard, dogs not allowed.

**Praa Sands**
Popular beach, lifeguard, dogs not allowed.

Lifeguards, where indicated, are on summer service. Dogs are not allowed on several popular beaches from Easter Day to September. During winter, when dogs are allowed, owners must use poop scoops.

### BOAT TRIPS

**Falmouth**
Prince of Wales Pier. Regular passenger ferries to St Mawes and Flushing. River cruises to Roseland Peninsula and Truro. Sea cruises.

### BOWLING

Falmouth Bowling Club, Penryn. For further information please contact the local Tourist Information Centre.

### CYCLING

A network of quiet lanes offers good cycling between the main roads and main centres. Cycling is not permitted on public footpaths or on the coast path.

### CYCLE HIRE

**Mullion**
Atlantic Forge. Tel: 01326 240294.

### GOLF COURSES

**Falmouth**
Falmouth Golf Club, Swanpool Road. Tel: 01326 311262.

**Helston**
Helston Golf and Leisure. Tel: 01326 565103.

**Mawnan Smith**
Budock Vean Golf and Country Club. Tel: 01326 252100.

**Mullion**
Mullion Golf Club, Cury. Tel: 01326 240685.

### HORSE-RIDING

**Helston**
Nanfan Farm Riding Stables, Cury. Tel: 01326 240413.

### SAILING

**Falmouth**
Falmouth School of Sailing. Tel: 01326 211311.

**St Anthony**
Anthony Jenkins. Tel: 01326 231357.

### WATERSPORTS

**Coverack**
Coverack Windsurfing Centre. Tel: 01326 280939.

**Stithians Lake**
Between Falmouth and Helston off the A394. Tel: 01209 860301. Open Easter–Oct & weekends in winter.

## Annual Events and Customs

Gig racing, once a serious quest for business, is now a major sport in Cornwall. Many villages and towns have their own gigs. Races are held throughout the summer at such venues as Cadgwith and Porthleven.

**Falmouth**
Falmouth Regatta Week. August. Maritime events including racing of traditional oyster boats.

**Helston**
Helston Flora Day. 8 May, or previous Saturday if 8 May is a Sunday or Monday. The famous Furry Dance. Several dances throughout day starting at 7am. Market stalls.

# The Land's End Peninsula: St Ives and Penzance and The Isles of Scilly

Cornwall's 'First and Last' peninsula is a vivid, atmospheric landscape of spectacular cliffs and golden beaches that are washed by the clear Atlantic waters. Inland, small fields and narrow, twisting lanes lie embedded within a network of granite hedges that are smothered with wild flowers. Prehistoric monuments stand amidst the heather and pale grass of the moorland hills and the rugged north coast is noted for the industrial archaeology of its abandoned tin mines. The main towns of St Ives and Penzance have contrasting, yet complementary appeal, and the varied rural and coastal communities mix the atmosphere of Old Cornwall with an engaging flavour of Mediterranean France.

## HAYLE  Map ref SW5537

Hayle's industrial past was sustained by Victorian tin and copper mining, reflected in such local names as Copperhouse and Foundry. Today, Hayle's rather straggling extent and its historical decline have denied it picturesque appeal; but awareness of the town's industrial past makes a visit rewarding for those looking for the history under the skin. A walk along the eastern side of the harbour and along the northern side of the large tidal pond of Copperhouse Pool, though not entirely scenic, is worthwhile. The contrast between the dereliction of Hayle's harbour area and the spaciousness and brightness of its nearby beaches is startling. Access to several miles of beach can be gained from Hayle by following the road through the village of Phillack and out to a car park amidst shoals of chalets. The town has good shops, galleries and craft shops, restaurants and several down-to-earth pubs.

### BIRDS OF A FEATHER

Hayle Estuary is an important winter feeding ground for wild birds, a bonus to bird-watchers in spring and autumn especially. Some very rare sightings are possible during autumn migrations when vagrant species from America may be pushed off their north-to-south migratory path and driven across the Atlantic to Cornwall. The best site is at Lelant Saltings to the west of Hayle. Access is from just off the A30 on the Penzance and St Ives road by the Old Quay House Inn.

*Look beyond Hayle to its wonderful beaches of golden sand*

Lurid tales of the deliberate wrecking of sailing ships in Cornwall are dubious. False 'guiding' lights on cliffs during storms would hardly be seen by desperate seamen. But wrecks were fair game for poverty-stricken communities and there was violence between wreckers and coastguards, especially when tubs of spirit were rolling up the beaches. But the promise of more essential goods lay behind the wrecking frenzy of a deprived people. As recently as the mid 1980s, several containers of tobacco were washed up near St Just. Although the unseasoned tobacco was fairly acrid, old Cornish recipes for mellowing the leaves were resurrected and sackloads of tobacco disappeared across the fields.

*Granite from Lamorna Cove was used for building lighthouses*

## LAMORNA  Map ref SW4424

Lamorna is the most sheltered of the narrow valleys that lead gently down to the south-facing shores of Mount's Bay. The road that leads down Lamorna Valley is narrow and can become congested during Bank Holidays. It is a delightful road nonetheless, descending through shady woodland to reach an unexpected bay that is fringed by granite cliffs. This is Lamorna's theme; there is charm around every corner if you are willing to explore. Granite from Lamorna's hillside quarries was used to build many Victorian lighthouses and such famous features as the Thames Embankment. On the way down to the cove is the Wink Inn, a classic Cornish pub with an engaging atmosphere. The 'wink' signifies the blind eye that the gentry and local vicars often turned to old-time smuggling. Lamorna's rugged granite quay is a pleasant place to linger.

About a mile (1.6km) west of Lamorna Valley in a field alongside the B3315 is a stone circle of the early Bronze Age – the famous Rosemodress, or Boleigh Circle of 19 upright stones. It is popularly known as the Merry Maidens, from entertaining but ridiculous legends of young girls turned to stone for dancing on a Sunday. In nearby fields are two tall standing stones, the Pipers, who suffered the same fate. They are all more likely to have been ceremonial sites of the Bronze-Age peoples. A short distance west of the Merry Maidens, and close to the road, is the Tregiffian entrance grave of the early Bronze Age, comprising a kerbed cairn with a chamber roofed with slabs.

### LAND'S END  Map ref SW3425

The symbolic geography of Land's End demands a visit although the natural attractions of the area are perhaps best enjoyed outside the busiest holiday periods. Do not expect to find yourselves romantically alone during daylight hours – except in a Force 9 gale.

But while rugged weather may enhance the Land's End Experience for the true romantic, the venue's numerous covered attractions are enjoyable as wet-weather alternatives. They include exhibitions, gift shops, craft centres and galleries, and the 'Last Labyrinth' electronic theatre where the real experiences of the Cornish coast are cleverly, if sometimes ironically, simulated. There is a choice of eating places within the complex and the Land's End Hotel is in a splendid position overlooking the Longships Lighthouse. There may be car-queues on the approach on popular Bank Holidays and during peak holiday periods.

Open access on foot, of course, is time-honoured and for those who prefer a more robust approach than by car, the coast path can be followed to Land's End from Sennen in the north (1 mile/1.6km) or from Porthgwarra in the south-east (3 miles/4.8km).

### MARAZION  Map ref SW5130

Marazion is a town first and foremost. You may earn yourself a deservedly frosty glance if you call this ancient borough anything less. It was the main trading port of Mount's Bay until an upstart Penzance developed its own markets and port during the 16th century. But

*High cliffs at Land's End*

#### END-TO-ENDERS

The long walk from John O' Groats, at the northern tip of Scotland, to Land's End has attracted a multitude of people eager to cover the 603 miles (970km) in one piece. Famous End-to-Enders include Ian Botham and Jimmy Saville. Some began anonymously and then became famous, like the round-the-world walker Ffyona Campbell. Most make the trip for personal reasons, or for charities, which have benefited hugely from such efforts. There is an official End-to-Enders Club.

Straightforward walking remains the obvious challenge, but there have been numerous variations from four-wheels to two wheels, bed-pushes, to nude cyclists (but only for the last few sunny Cornish miles). A few determined souls have done it via the coast.

**DISHY FISH**

Pilchards are not so easy to come by these days, but a good Cornish fish merchant will have a splendid selection of fish to tempt you. Mackerel are a good fleshy fish, though oily; the old Cornish treatment was to 'souse' them in vinegar and bay leaves, but today smoked and peppered mackerel are available. And very tasty too. Hake, cod, haddock and ling are all meaty, flavourful fish. Best of all is John Dory and turbot. Expensive Dover and Lemon sole will tempt the taste, but test the treasury. Monkfish is good for imaginative cooking. *Bon appetit*!

*The tidal island of St Michael's Mount is visible from Marazion to Penzance*

Marazion has remained as distinctive as its lovely name which derives, rather plainly, from the Cornish word for market. There is an informative little museum at the town hall in Market Square and there are antique and craft shops, pleasant pubs, restaurants and cafés. Marazion Beach offers safe bathing and is a sun trap. It has a reputation for good windsurfing especially during spring and autumn, when conditions are breezy. The quiet village of Perranuthnoe, a short distance south-east with a south-facing beach also provides reasonable surfing at times. A few miles further east lies Prussia Cove, a secluded rocky inlet of great charm reached most rewardingly by a 2-mile (3.2km) walk along the coast path.

The great complement to Marazion is the castellated St Michael's Mount (National Trust), the most romantic offshore island in Britain and a matching image to Mont St Michel off the Normandy coast. The Mount was dedicated to St Michael after claims of miraculous sightings of the saint by 5th-century fishermen. Even today shafts of celestial light seem drawn to St Michael's Mount although a view of angels is perhaps less likely. In its day the Mount has been monastery, prison, and castle-under-siege. The Mount is nicely defined as a part-time island by successive high tides during which it may be reached by a pleasant boat trip. At low tide the approach is on foot along a fine cobbled causeway.

## MOUSEHOLE   Map ref SW4626

Quaintness clings to Mousehole's name like a cat. But 'Mouz'l', as it should be pronounced, is a fishing village of strong character, even though the days are long gone when its harbour was crammed with pilchard fishing boats. The name derives from obscure roots. Its old Cornish name is *Porth Enys*, meaning 'the landing place by the island'. The small island offshore from Mousehole is called St Clement's after a hermit who is said to have maintained a warning light there.

Tempting alleyways and passages wriggle between sturdy cottages in Mousehole and the harbourside Ship Inn rounds things off with a flourish. The far end of Mousehole's tiny harbour has a splendid inner wall of irregular granite blocks, perfect for imaginative photography or sketching. There are some shops, including craft shops, cafés and restaurants. Mousehole was not built for the motor car and is best explored on foot. There is a car park by the harbour but it fills quickly during busy periods. The other is just outside the village on the approach from Newlyn.

A steep hill leads inland from Mousehole to the village of Paul where the Church of St Pol de Leon has some impressive features. These include a memorial to the Mousehole crew of the local lifeboat, the *Solomon Browne*. They died heroically near Lamorna during an appalling storm in December 1981 after repeated attempts to save the eight people aboard the crew of the wrecked cargo vessel *Union Star*. The road out of Mousehole to the west leads up the dauntingly steep Raginnis Hill. Part way up is the famous Mousehole Bird Hospital, a refuge for countless injured birds many of which are the victims of oil pollution. The recovery cages often contain several very vocal birds.

*A narrow entrance from the sea protects the boats in Mousehole harbour*

### SUPERSTITIONS

Superstition is still in good health in Cornwall, especially in the fishing industry. Bad luck omens are numerous and seem inexplicable in many cases. They may have developed as targets of blame for ill fortune in an industry at risk from danger and unpredictable weather. Never, ever mention to a fisherman rabbits, vicars, nuns, foxes, donkeys, salmon or three-cornered sandwiches. They signify the worst kind of luck. Never whistle on the quayside, lest you encourage the wind. Avoid the colour green. Don't take a Cornish pasty on a boat, unless you have broken off both ends so that the wind can blow through it. And never stir your tea anti-clockwise in a quayside café or you may stir up a storm. When aboard a boat, touch 'cold iron' rather than wood to ward off bad luck.

*The tall chimneys of former mines still pierce the skies at Pendeen as a reminder of its industrial past*

---

**PREHISTORIC PEDAL**
*A cycle ride to ancient monuments — 20 miles (32km), mostly moderate with some steep gradients.*
From Penzance, take the A30 west to Drift; turn right and pass Drift Reservoir then keep ahead following signs for 'Brane' and 'Carn Euny'. Visit Carn Euny Iron-Age village on foot, then retrace your route and follow signs to Sancreed. Turn left beyond Sancreed church; continue to St Just then follow the B3306 north to Pendeen. Beyond Pendeen, go left, signed 'Pendeen Lighthouse'. After ½ mile (0.8km) go right to Pendeen Manor Farm and, with permission, view the Iron-Age underground chamber. Return to the B3306 and continue left to Morvah. Turn right beyond Morvah, signed *(continued on next page)*

**PENDEEN**   Map ref SW3834
Pendeen is made up of a straggling line of small communities that were linked to tin and copper mines on the north coast of the Land's End peninsula. The smaller villages of Carnyorth, Trewellard, Boscaswell and Bojewyan make up the roll call of this last of Cornwall's coastal mining communities. The area's appeal is based on the startling conjunction of a fractured mining landscape and the raw beauty of the Atlantic coast. Pendeen's Geevor Mine was the mainstay of the larger area but the mine closed in 1991 in the face of international market pressures, and in spite of a spirited campaign by local people to save the industry. Surface freehold of Geevor is now owned by Cornwall County Council and the complex is being imaginatively developed as a visitor centre.

Just south of Geevor is the National Trust's Levant Engine House which is reached from Trewellard. At Levant, the silken power of steam is harnessed to a restored working beam engine. Pendeen has craft and mineral shops.

**THE PENWITH MOORS**   Map ref SW4535
The Penwith Moors run parallel to the north coast of the Land's End peninsula through an undulating series of hills that are crowned with granite tors. The high ground begins at Rosewall Hill just west of St Ives and is continuous throughout the beautiful parishes of Zennor and Morvah. Smaller areas of moorland continue the westward-leading sequence to Chapel Carn Brea above the wide, flat coastal plateau of Land's End itself. The moorland is a splendid counterpoint to the peninsula's outstanding coastline and is easily accessible from a number of points. The Penwith Moors are noted for their ecological value and for their unique concentration of Neolithic, Bronze-Age and Iron-Age remains that include

burial chambers, settlements, stone circles and standing stones. Most of the northern moors are at the heart of the Government-designated Environmentally Sensitive Area within which farmers are compensated for working in sympathy with the traditional structure of the ancient landscape.

## PENZANCE  Map ref SW4730

Penzance has a sunny, friendly character gained from its south-facing position on the most sheltered part of Mount's Bay and from the bustle of its attractive streets. It has the only promenade in Cornwall and it is a lengthy one, with wonderful views; best foot forward. The open-air, art deco Jubilee Swimming Pool rounds off the harbour end of the promenade. Penzance harbour is small but has a busy atmosphere and a mix of vessels from fishing boats to visiting yachts; the passenger boat to the Isles of Scilly (see page 115) leaves from the outer pier. The Trinity House National Lighthouse Centre, a fascinating museum of lighthouse and maritime history, is just by the harbour and the nearby Barbican Centre has good craft shops.

A pleasant approach to the harbour, from the busy Market Place, is down the diverting Chapel Street where there are antique and craft shops, pubs and eating houses and a Maritime Museum. Penzance's attractive main street, Market Jew Street, is enhanced further by a raised granite terrace. There are shops of all kinds here, and in the pedestrianised Causewayhead that leads inland from Market Place. Towards the sea, and to either side of the Morrab Road, are Morrab Gardens and Penlee Park; the former is a lovely ornamental garden, the latter houses the Penlee House Gallery and Museum with its delightfully placed orangery café. Another fine attraction is the Geological Museum in the mightily imposing St John's Hall, one of the largest granite buildings in the world.

'Madron' with steep climb and descent to Bosullow. Opposite Men-an-Tol Studio, a track leads to Men-an-Tol, a probable remnant of a prehistoric burial chamber. From Bosullow follow the road to reach Lanyon Quoit. Return to Penzance through Madron.

### HIGH PLACES

North-east of Sennen, the ground rises to Chapel Carn Brea, a smooth-browed hill cared for by the National Trust and reached by turning off the A30 Land's End road at Crows-an-wra. There is a small car park by the road side from which a path leads to the summit of this airy hill. At various times in the past, Chapel Carn Brea was the site of a Bronze-Age burial chamber, a medieval chapel and a beacon.

*Market Jew Street, with its statue of Sir Humphry Davy, lies at the very heart of Penzance*

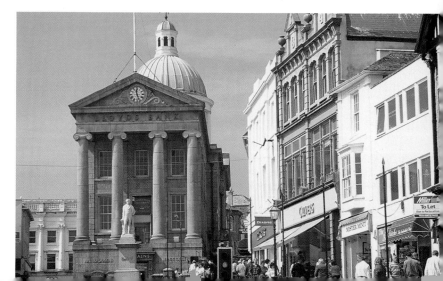

**THE MINERS' FRIEND**
Humphry Davy was born in Market Jew Street, Penzance in 1778 and died in Geneva in 1829. He was apprenticed at 17 to a Penzance doctor, John Bingham Borlase, and later moved to Bristol where he was soon recognised as an outstanding chemist. Davy is credited with discovering that chemical compounds can be broken down into their elements through electrolysis. In this way he discovered such important elements as calcium, magnesium, barium and potassium. His most famous invention was the miners' safety lamp, for which he never took out a patent on the grounds that, without the restriction of a patent, use of the lamp would become widespread.

*The Neolithic tomb of Lanyon Quoit lies just outside Penzance, near Madron*

To the west, Penzance merges with Newlyn, the major fishing port in the south-west. Newlyn harbour is full of life and colour. Scores of fishing boats of all types and sizes work from here in spite of the increasing difficulties of the modern international industry. The large fish market bustles with activity in the early morning as boats land a remarkable variety of fish. Parking at Newlyn is difficult, and most visitors find that a walk along Penzance's spacious promenade and on along the seafront to Newlyn is a pleasant alternative, which can be combined with a visit to the Newlyn Art Gallery along the way.

Just outside Penzance is the National Trust's Trengwainton Garden, a complex of five walled gardens amidst mature woodland. Trengwainton is at its best during spring and early summer, with an exquisite display of magnolias, acacias, camellias and azaleas as well as its splendid rhododendrons. The garden can be reached via Heamoor, or from Tremethick Cross on the St Just road.

Penzance has a summer festival called Golowan that derives from the celebratory lighting of fires on Midsummer Eve, which is also St John's Eve. The festival lasts for two weeks in mid-June and involves numerous cultural events and entertainment. It culminates in Mazey Day when the streets of Penzance are closed to traffic and the main street, Market Jew Street, is decked out with greenery and hosts a street fair. There are lively processions by local children and a boisterous Serpent Dance with much music and fun.

## PORTHCURNO  Map ref SW3822

The golden sand of Porthcurno's beaches and the clarity of its sea supports Cornwall's claim to be an alternative to the Mediterranean. Under a blazing summer sun, the comparison is apt. Granite towers and pinnacles lie embedded in the steep vegetated slopes that encircle the bay and the sand lies deeply against the shoreline. Some of the adjoining beaches are covered at high tide but the main Porthcurno beach is always available, clean, sparkling and luxurious.

For many years Porthcurno was the centre of international cable telegraphy. From here, undersea telegraph cables communicated with the rest of the world and, at one time, the Cable and Wireless Company ran a training college in the Porthcurno Valley. In 1994, Porthcurno beach and its adjacent cliff land was given to the National Trust by the company, which had relocated its training facilities to Coventry. There is a fascinating telegraph museum housed in underground chambers within the old Porthcurno college complex just inland from the large car park.

The visitor to Porthcurno is spoiled for choice. The main beach is marvellously persuasive for wriggling the toes; but to either side lie lovely coastal walks. Eastward is the famous Logan Rock, a vast monolith that once rocked at the touch of a finger but is less responsive now, and westward is the Minack Theatre, Porth Chapel beach and the little Church of St Levan. St Levan can also be reached along the narrow road that climbs steeply uphill from Porthcurno. There is a car park by St Levan Church. All around Porthcurno Bay you will find lovely coves, such as Penberth, and exquisite tidal beaches, and the eastern side is flanked by the magnificent headland of Treryn Dinas (see Walk on page 106).

### THEATRE ON THE CLIFFS

The Minack Theatre above Porthcurno perches on the edge of rough, red-gold cliffs on the western arm of the bay. It was the life's work of Rowena Cade who began her labour of love in the 1920s and with dedicated assistants designed and helped build this sun-drenched theatre that seems to grow out of the natural rock. There is a popular exhibition centre and a coffee shop. During the summer season plays and musicals are staged against the most spectacular backdrop in British Theatre. Dolphins make impromptu appearances in the bay below; brightly-lit fishing boats steal through the dusk. At times fog, wind and rain contribute their own special Cornish effects. Bring wine for soft summer evenings, hot chocolate otherwise; a memorable night out, either way.

*The Minack Theatre makes the most of its cliffside setting*

# Cliff Theatre and Cliff Castle

This exhilarating walk leads to Porthcurno and an underground telegraphy museum, then to a beautiful old church, returning past golden beaches, a cliffside theatre and a magnificent promontory. Good paths, but rocky in parts, with a few very steep sections.

Time: 2½ hours. Distance: 3½ miles (5.6km).
Location: 7 miles (11.3km) south-west of Penzance.
Start: Treen car park at Treen village, about 2 miles (3.2km) south of St Buryan, off the B3315. (OS grid ref: SW395229).
OS Maps: Landranger 203 (Land's End, The Lizard and Isles of Scilly) 1:50,000.
Explorer 102 (Land's End) 1:25,000.
See Key to Walks on page 121.

### ROUTE DIRECTIONS

From the car park turn left onto a rough lane, following it for half a mile (0.8km) to reach the coast path. Turn right, then in 50 yards (46m) bear right along a path. Soon pass between old pill-boxes, and then pass a gate and some large boulders at a path

*Sea-rippled sand on the beach at Treen*

junction. Keep ahead and descend into Porthcurno Valley. Turn right at a junction with a track that leads to **Porthcurno** Beach and reach a large car park. Turn right from its top exit, proceed up the road for 300 yards (274m), then turn sharp left on to a wide track just past the Porthcurno Hotel. In 80 yards (73m) go through a gate and continue to a stone stile into an open yard by cottages. Cross to the far corner of the open area to a kissing gate. Continue to St Levan Church, passing a granite cross on the way.

Enter the churchyard via a splendid stile and walk either way round the church leaving by the south gate onto a lane. Take the track opposite, cross a stream and shortly keep left at a junction, eventually joining the coast path. Keep ahead past St Levan's Well and descend to cross a footbridge.

Follow the coast path steeply uphill, cross the neck of **Pedn-mên-an-mere**, and soon reach the car park of the **Minack Open Air Theatre**. Keep left of the Minack Theatre entrance down a surfaced track and then descend steeply twisting steps. (These steps are very steep. The less agile may find it easier to follow the exit road from the Minack car park, and then the public road, with care, down right to Porthcurno.)

Below the steep steps, the path levels off, then after 400 yards (366m), bear right at a fork, to reach a junction with the beach track from Porthcurno car park. Cross over and take the track opposite, signed 'Penberth'. (If the road descent is taken, go through the car park and follow the beach track to this point).

Climb very steeply to the cliff-top, passing a wooden navigation mast and a pill-box on the right, then at a T-junction (passed previously), turn right and continue past the two old pill boxes. In 60 yards (55m) fork right and continue round the cliff-top, passing a pyramid-shaped memorial.

In 300 yards (274m) at a junction of several paths, take the first path right, then keep right at the next junction of paths. In 30 yards (27m) reach a further crossing of paths by a granite NT marker. (The headland of **Treryn Dinas, and the Logan Rock** can be reached by turning right through the gap in the obvious embankment ahead). On the main route, turn left past NT marker to a stile, then follow field paths over several stiles for the return to Treen and the car park.

### POINTS OF INTEREST

**Porthcurno**
Famed for its golden beach, matching granite cliffs, and sea of Mediterranean blue. The Porthcurno Valley is also known for its historic telecommunication links.

There is a fascinating Telegraph Museum just above the Porthcurno car park.

**Pedn-mân-an-mere**
This headland sports the remains of an old radio mast erected in 1902 by the Eastern Telegraph Company, a commercial rival of the Marconi Company. The ETC always claimed that the radio aerials on the mast were for legitimate transmissions. But their true purpose was industrial espionage.

**Minack Open Air Theatre**
The Minack was developed by the late Miss Rowena Cade, who began her classically inspired project in the 1920s. The theatre is open to visitors at certain times when plays are not being performed.

**Treryn Dinas and Logan Rock**
This great headland is known popularly as Logan Rock because of the 60-ton boulder that crowns the inner ramparts and once rocked, at the touch of a finger.

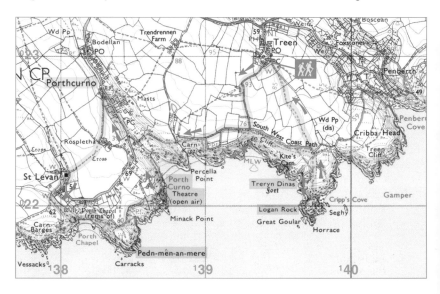

**ART FROM THE HEARTLAND**
A pleasant day can be spent visiting the main art galleries of the Land's End peninsula. The St Ives Tate displays paintings by leading artists of the St Ives School, and the associated Barbara Hepworth Museum is a unique celebration of the work and the working environment of one of Britain's most significant sculptors. The Penwith Gallery and the St Ives Society of Arts Gallery, both in St Ives, also show good local work. Penzance Gallery features the earlier Newlyn School and the Newlyn Gallery has emerged as a lively exhibition space for contemporary art as well as a showcase for the work of local artists. There are also numerous commercial galleries throughout the peninsula.

*Narrow lanes wind between
the houses of St Ives*

## PORTHGWARRA  Map ref SW3721

Porthgwarra lies to the west of Porthcurno and is sheltered from the prevailing Atlantic winds by high ground that culminates at the magnificent granite cliff of Chair Ladder at Gwennap Head, the most southerly extent of the Land's End peninsula. At Porthgwarra, tunnels have been carved through the softer rock of flanking promontories to allow access to the beach by donkey and trap in the days when seaweed was collected by neighbouring farmers to fertilise their fields. The cliff-top walks to the west are magnificent and the area is noted for rare species of birds that often make landfall here during spring and autumn migrations.

## ST IVES  Map ref SW5140

St Ives' rare character springs from its fishing traditions, its artistic inheritance, and its tourism industry. There is a clash of style between all three at times, but St Ives has survived such competing interests. Not only is the town the archetypal Cornish fishing port but it has magnificent beaches of silken sand that offer both safe family bathing and surf to sing about. The town has aimed determinedly up-market in recent years and has benefited greatly from the St Ives Tate Gallery which opened in 1993. The gallery stands above the spectacular Porthmeor Beach, its curves and crests as white as the waves below. The paintings on display are by leading contemporaries of the St Ives School including Patrick Heron, Peter Lanyon and Terry Frost. It is a joy to find such paintings within the very landscape that inspired them. The view to seaward from the gallery's roof terrace is worth crossing the world for. Before The Tate opened, The Barbara Hepworth Museum and Sculpture Garden was the most important artistic attraction here and still remains popular.

But St Ives is a delight overall because of its narrow, canyon-like streets, ubiquitous granite cobbles, and clear, sea-mirrored light. The parish church of St Ia is one of the finest in Cornwall. St Ives harbour area, known locally as 'Downlong', is a maze of exquisite vernacular granite buildings where you catch satisfying glimpses of shady courtyards and passageways. And always those bright beaches to escape to; Porthminster to the south, sheltered and calm; Porthmeor to the north, a more lively surfing beach.

There are smaller beaches at the harbour and in the lee of the Island, the breezy, green promontory that juts out to sea from a low-lying neck of land. The price of all this is potential overcrowding at the busiest holiday periods. Avoid dawdling through St Ives by car and be prepared for close-quarters humanity in the narrow Fore Street and along the busy harbour front. There is a park-and-ride scheme at Trenwith above the town and another at Lelant Station, south east of the town, which uses a little branch line. Artistic ambience – and, at times, pretension – means that St Ives has numerous galleries and craft shops. There is an excellent town museum at Wheal Dream, and most of the numerous restaurants and pubs are of quality and character.

*The clear light at St Ives has long attracted artists, including Turner*

### TRENCROM HILL

The fine rocky hill of Trencrom, the site of an Iron-Age encampment, stands above the Hayle Estuary and can be reached from Lelant or from the B3311 St Ives to Penzance road. Trencrom is in the care of the National Trust and there is a small car park on its southern side. The path to the summit is short and steep in places, but the views are outstanding. Just west of Trencrom is the little village of Nancledra from where the green and peaceful Towednack Valley runs north to the sea through a gap in the coastal hills.

# A Famous Mining Coast

*An absorbing walk along the famous tin-mining coast of St Just and Botallack, passing numerous mining remains. Generally level along cliff-tops but with some steep climbs and descents. Quite rocky in places.*

Time: 3½ hours. Distance: 7 miles (11.3km).
Location: 7 miles (11.3km) west of Penzance.
Start: Free car park in Market Street in St Just, off the A3071.
(OS grid ref: SW369313).
OS Maps: Landranger 203 (Land's End, The Lizard and Isles of Scilly) 1:50,000.
Explorer 102 (Land's End) 1:25,000.
See Key to Walks on page 121.

## ROUTE DIRECTIONS

From the car park exit opposite the public library, turn left, then left again along Bosorne Terrace, and keep ahead at a junction. Where the road curves left at another junction, keep right. After ¼ mile (0.4km), bear right at the road end onto a rough track, which soon narrows to a path. Keep right at a fork, then turn right along a road, heading uphill to some houses.

Bear sharply left at a junction by the houses on to a surfaced lane for 300 yards (274m) to a house, then keep straight on along a path, keeping left where it forks. Keep ahead towards a mine chimneystack, turn left onto a road passing the stack and later pass **Ballowall Barrow** ancient burial chamber.

Where the road ends, continue down a stony track alongside a golf course, following it right, then go sharp left at a junction by an acorn signpost and continue to the rim of Priest's Cove. Bear right up a flight of steps to a road above Cape Cornwall. Turn right, then in 150 yards (137m) above the car park entrance, turn left along a stony track, signed 'Pendeen Watch'. Keep left at a fork just past a solitary house, then in 400 yards (365m) go left at the next fork. Descend a steep, rocky path into the valley bottom. Bear right at a junction near a renovated pond, and continue to a footbridge, then on reaching a T-junction with a track, turn left. Almost immediately, take a path on your left and soon reach a junction with a path leading uphill to the right. Do not take this path just yet. Instead, continue straight ahead down the Nancherrow Valley to **Porth Ledden** Cove. Retrace your steps back to the junction and follow the path uphill, enjoying fine views to **Cape Cornwall**. At a broad track, turn left, then just before the track curves right, bear off right, by a stone 'Coast Path' sign , to a stile. Proceed ahead past ruined buildings to your left, following a grassy track to a stile, and turn left onto a stony track.

Keep left at a fork by a ruined mine building on the left, then at another fork, abreast of a single chimney stack, bear left downhill to reach **The Crowns** mine buildings. Retrace your steps and, at the junction below the single chimney stack, turn left with the coast path to reach a junction and a broad track. Turn right, pass buildings and a long, single-storeyed house, then bear right at a wide junction by an old barn, to follow a track for ¼ mile (0.4km) to where it merges with a track by the ruined mine buildings passed previously. Keep ahead, curve left then keep right at a fork and turn left at the next junction. The track soon merges with a surfaced road by Kenidjack Farm. Proceed

*Old mines hug the cliffs at Botallack*

for ¼ mile (0.4km), then turn right and cross a wooden footbridge. Follow the defined path over stiles and through small fields to an alleyway and the edge of St Just.

Turn right along the road signed 'Cape Cornwall', pass the Methodist church and continue to a junction. Cross slightly right, bear left along West Place, then turn left into Market Street to the car park.

### POINTS OF INTEREST

**Ballowall Barrow**
A remarkable example of an Early Bronze-Age burial chamber of about 4,000 years ago.

**Porth Ledden**
Porth Ledden marks the seaward end of the Nancherrow Valley, the scene of intensive mining activity last century and a rich storehouse of mining artefacts. The large granite edifice at the mouth of the valley is the wheel pit of Wheal Call mine. It housed a giant water wheel that fed power to the valley mine workings.

**Cape Cornwall**
This shapely promontory is the only 'cape' in England. A cape is a promontory marking the division between two oceans, or channels, in this case the English Channel and St George's Channel.

**The Crowns**
The refurbished mine buildings of the Crowns mine at Botallack, are famous symbols of Cornish coastal mining. The 19th-century workings extended for about a third of a mile (0.5km) under the seabed.

## THE MINING COAST

Tin mining is now at an end on the north coast of the Land's End Peninsula, but the spirit of this once great Cornish industry is still potent, not least in the self-awareness among local people of a past that is a mix of achievement and of tragedy. The exquisitely beautiful landscape in which coastal mining took place has blurred the worst excesses of industry, and today the National Trust, with the help and expertise of local people is preserving the proudest symbols of mining while protecting the vulnerable ecology of this Atlantic coast.

*The handsome parish church dominates a corner of St Just's market square*

## ST JUST  Map ref SW3731

There is a generous Market Square at the heart of this sturdy Cornish town. At the eastern corner of the square stands the parish church, a 15th-century building in good weathered granite, with a handsome interior. Market Square has a number of friendly pubs and there are cafés and a good selection of shops within the square and in the streets that radiate from it. St Just is the ideal base from which to explore the famous mining coast of the Land's End peninsula.

The elegant headland of Cape Cornwall lies to the west; it is rugged, yet shapely and its rounded summit is crowned with the chimney stack of a long defunct mine. On the southern edge of the cape is Priest's Cove from where small fishing boats work. From the cove, a stony track leads up to the rocky headland of Carn Gloose from where the impressive burial chamber of Ballowall lies about 150 yards (137m) inland. (see Walk on page 110). The cape, and a large extent of coastline to either side, is in the care of the National Trust.

To the north lies the remarkable mining area of Kenidjack and the Nancherrow Valley, a historic mining landscape that is being skilfully preserved by the Trust. A mile north of the town along the B3306 is the village of Botallack and the nearby coastal area is particularly rich in old mine buildings.

## SENNEN  Map ref SW3525

The Atlantic truly begins at Sennen's Whitesand Bay where the west-facing beaches can be exhilarating when the surf is high. Gwenver Beach to the north is a 'serious' surfing and body boarding beach that is also delightful for soaking up the sun, though close attention should be paid to safety flags and to lifeguards. Tidal currents can be fierce. Sennen Beach is the larger of the two. It is less adventurous but just as delightful and is easily accessible from the car park at Sennen Cove.

Sennen is in two halves. The village proper is on the higher ground alongside the A30. Sennen Cove has the main attractions of the beaches and of fine granite cliffs to the south. A car park at the far end gives access to the cliff path and to Land's End on foot. This southern end of the cove spills into the ocean and has a brisk sea-going atmosphere with a narrow quay edging into the sea – to be avoided during rough conditions – and a lifeboat house with a smart modern lifeboat. The nearby wood and granite Round House contained the capstan that was used for hauling boats out of the water. It is now an excellent craft shop and gallery.

*Sennen is the westernmost village of mainland Britain*

**A SCENIC ROUTE**
One of the finest scenic drives in England is to the north of Sennen along the B3306 coast road. The section between Morvah and St Ives is quite spectacular. The road winds its sinuous way between mottled moorland and the patchworked web of Iron-Age fields that cluster together along the narrow coastal plateau above a glittering sea. There are pubs along the way and several cream-tea havens.

## GURNARD'S HEAD

Just over a mile to the west of Zennor Head lies the even more stupendous Gurnard's Head, a long elegant promontory that rises to a great gnarled headland ringed with sheer black cliffs. There are remains of embankments across the neck of this Iron-Age site and on the flanking slopes are the rough remains of Iron-Age houses. Gurnard's Head may be reached from the B3306, at the Gurnard's Head Hotel, a mile south west of Zennor but parking is limited. The coast path between Zennor Head and Gurnard's Head makes for a pleasantly rough walk of about 1½ miles (2.4km). Both headlands are in the care of the National Trust.

*The inn by the church at Zennor was a favourite haunt of D H Lawrence*

## ZENNOR  Map ref SW4538

At Zennor, rough tawny hills slope down towards the echoing sea cliffs. Between hills and sea lies a narrow coastal plateau of small irregular fields whose Cornish 'hedges' of rough granite date from the Iron Age. Because of its antiquity this still-farmed landscape has earned Zennor protected status for ecological and archaeological reasons. Such vulnerability should be taken into account when visiting Zennor and its surrounding countryside. Below the car park is the Wayside Museum; it is crammed with fascinating exhibits and information about farming, mining, archaeology and folklore. Zennor's Church of St Senara lords it rather handsomely over the village.

Zennor has a myth of a mermaid – the story is a touch overplayed, but it is endearing. The mermaid was said to have seduced a local chorister into the dark waters below the lofty Zennor Head. Who could blame either of them? On quiet evenings, the smooth heads of seals perpetuate the legend and an attractive bench-end motif in Zennor Church encourages the mermaid's tale.

Access to Zennor Head and to the coast path is on foot down a narrow lane that starts behind the Tinner's Arms. Zennor Head has a flat top, but its western flank is spectacular. Towering cliffs fall darkly into a narrow gulf, the sea crashes white against the shoreline far below, the sense of space and distance is overpowering. If you can tear yourself away from thoughts of mermaids, it is an invigorating 6 miles (9.6km) walk eastwards to St Ives along some of the most remote coastline in Cornwall.

## THE ISLES OF SCILLY Map ref SV9111

The Isles of Scilly are famously known as the 'Fortunate Islands' or the 'Sunshine Islands'. They deserve the superlatives, though their beauty and uniqueness require no exaggeration. The hundred or so islands and islets that make up the archipelago lie 28 miles (45km) west-south-west of Land's End as the seagull flies. Only five are inhabited – St Mary's, St Agnes, St Martin's, Bryher and Tresco – and they offer a rare combination of glorious seascapes, golden beaches and crystal-clear sea, with quiet green corners inland.

**Bryher**   Bryher lies amidst the north-western group of islands that include Tresco. It is 1½ miles (2.4km) long and barely half a mile (0.8km) across at its widest point. Bryher faces Tresco across the narrow channel of New Grimsby Sound and island life is focused on the beaches that fringe the Sound. Here boats draw up at a granite quay, or at the jetty, built as one of Anneka Rice's famous 'challenges' to extend landing times on Bryher and now known engagingly as 'Annequay'.

**St Agnes**   Just over a mile (1.6km) wide, St Agnes has a special atmosphere of serenity. It is the most southerly of the group and is separated from St Mary's by the deep water channel of St Mary's Sound. The Turk's Head and the Post Office are at the hub of the community. To the east the main island is linked by a narrow sandbar to the smaller tidal 'island' of Gugh and off its western shore is the protected bird island of Annet. Beyond Annet lie the dramatic reefs known as the Western Rocks that terminate at the Bishop Rock Lighthouse.

*The well-trodden Troy Town Maze at St Agnes*

**BEST BOAT TRIPS IN BRITAIN?**

Scillonians are outstanding seamen, and the great tradition of small-boat handling is maintained by the fishermen and by the boatmen who run pleasure trips. These boat trips are an essential part of getting the best from Scilly. The inter-island launches connect daily to St Mary's and also make trips between the islands. Some of the finest trips are those to the off-lying uninhabited islands and to the marine wildernesses of the Western Rocks, the Norrard Rocks and the Eastern Isles, where puffins and other seabirds can be seen at close quarters and where seals lie at their ease on sea-sucked ledges.

**LIVE AND LIVELY ENTERTAINMENT**
Entertainment on the Isles of Scilly is of a richly traditional nature. There are numerous slide shows and delightful talks in the local community hall of each islands. Island boatmen especially, are noted for their salty wit. Cricket is popular, and visitors are often press-ganged into making up teams, of often extremely competent islanders, in matches against mainland elevens. Don't even think of mentioning mid-on or mid-off.

**St Martin's**  The most northerly island in the group, St Martin's is 2 miles (3.2km) in length and just over half a mile (0.8km) wide. Landing on St Martin's can be adventurous at certain states of the tide, when walking the plank to reach the sandy shore from launches, becomes a necessity. Walking on St Martin's is exhilarating, though the lure of such magnificent beaches as Great Bay on St Martin's northern shore tends to distract.

**St Mary's**  St Mary's is the largest of the Isles of Scilly. Its main settlement of Hugh Town is the marine metropolis of the islands, and it is from Hugh Town Quay that the passenger launches leave for the exciting sea-trips that are an essential part of holidaying on Scilly. There are beaches on the north and south side of Hugh Town, the southern bay of Porth Cressa being particularly delightful. A footpath follows the coastline for a 9-mile (14.4km) circuit, passing several well-preserved prehistoric sites on the way. Early flower growing developed in Scilly from the late 1860s. Daffodils and narcissi are still exported from the islands, but the trade has declined in recent years.

**Tresco**  Tresco lies at the sheltered heart of the islands. It is more of a show-place than the rest of Scilly, a private domain where there is an atmosphere of carefully regulated life and of discreet pace. The exquisite sub-tropical gardens surrounding Tresco Abbey House are the main focus of the island. A priory to St Nicholas was established by Benedictine monks during the 12th century; the scant ruins which remain are now incorporated into the Abbey Gardens, where Burmese Honeysuckle, Australian Scarlet Bottle-brush, Aloes, Dracaenas, Mimosa, gigantic ice plants, and a host of other exotics line the terraced pathways. Tresco has a heliport from where connections can be made to Penzance. Dogs must always be kept on leads on Tresco.

*High walls and tall hedges shield the wind-blown fields of St Martin's*

# The Land's End Peninsula: St Ives and Penzance and the Isles of Scilly

Leisure Information
Places of Interest
Shopping
The Performing Arts
Sports, Activities and
the Outdoors
Annual Events and Customs

**Checklist**

## Leisure Information

### TOURIST INFORMATION CENTRES

**St Ives**
The Guildhall, Street-an-Pol.
Tel: 01209 611108.
**Penzance**
Station Road. Tel: 01209
611107.
**Hayle**
Putting Green, Lethlean Lane
(seasonal). Tel: 01209 611114.

### OTHER INFORMATION
**Coastguard**
Dial 999 and ask for the
Coastguard Service, which co-
ordinates rescue services.
**Cornwall Wildlife Trust**
Five Acres, Allet, Truro.
Tel: 01872 73939.
**English Heritage**
23 Savile Row, London.
Tel: 0171 973 3434.
**Health**
Information on health problems
is available Tel: 0800 665544.
Dental Helpline Tel: 0800
371192.
**Environment Agency**
Manley House, Kestrel Way,
Exeter.
Tel: 01392 444000.

**National Trust in Cornwall**
Regional Office, Lanhydrock,
Bodmin. Tel: 01208 74281.
**Parking**
Weekly permitsfor long stay car
parks are available from pay-
and-display machines.
There is a park and ride scheme
at Lelant Saltings Halt for the St
Ives Branch Line Railway.
**South West Water**
Highercombe Park, Lewdown,
Okehampton. Recreation/fishing
Tel: 01837 871565.
**Surf Call**
Tel: 0891 333080.
**Weather Call**
Tel: 0891 500758.

### ORDNANCE SURVEY MAPS
Explorer 1:25,000 Sheet 102.
Landranger 1:50,000 Sheet 203.

## Places of Interest

There will be an admission
charge unless otherwise stated.
**Barbara Hepworth Museum
and Sculpture Garden**
Barnoon Hill, St Ives. Tel: 01736
796226. Open all year, most
days. Combined admission with
Tate Gallery St Ives.
**Geevor Tin Mine**
Pendeen. Tel: 01736 788662.

Open all year, most days.
**Land's End**
Tel: 01736 871501. Open all
year, daily except Christmas.
**Levant Engine House**
Trewellard. Open Jul–Sep, most
days; rest of year certain days.
**Marazion Town Museum**
Town Hall, The Square. Open
daily during season.
**Minack Theatre and
Exhibition Centre**
Porthcurno. Theatre bookings
Tel: 01736 810181. Daytime
visits Tel: 01736 810098.
Theatre open end May to mid-
Sep. Exhibition Centre open
Mar–early Jan.
**National Lighthouse Centre**
Wharf Road, Penzance.
Tel: 01736 360077. Open
Apr–Oct, daily.
**Newlyn Art Gallery**
New Road, Newlyn, Penzance.
Tel: 01736 363715. Open all
year, most days.
**Penlee House Gallery and
Museum**
Penlee Park, Morrab Road. Tel:
01736 363625. Open all year,
most days.
**Penwith Society of Arts**
Back Road West, St Ives.
Tel: 01736 795579. Open all
year, most days.

**The Pilchard Works**
Newlyn, Penzance. Fishing museum and factory. Tel: 01736 332112. Open most days, Easter–Oct.

**Porthcurno Museum of Submarine Telegraphy**
Porthcurno. Tel: 01736 810966. Open weekdays mid-May to Oct.

**St Ives Museum**
Wheal Dream. Tel: 01736 796005. Open May–Oct, daily.

**St Ives Society of Artists**
The Old Mariners Church, Norway Square. Tel: 01736 795582.

**St Michael's Mount**
Marazion. Tel: 01736 710265. Open Apr–Oct, weekdays.

**Tate Gallery St Ives**
Porthmeor, St Ives. Tel: 01736 796226. Open all year, most days. Combined admission with Barbara Hepworth Museum.

**Trengwainton Garden**
Madron. Tel: 01736 363021. Open Mar–Oct, most days.

**Wayside Museum**
Zennor. Tel: 01736 796945. Open Easter–Oct, daily.

## SPECIAL INTEREST FOR CHILDREN

The following places may be of interest to visitors with children. Unless otherwise stated there will be an admission charge.

**Paradise Park**
Trelissick Road, Hayle. Tel: 01736 757407/753365. Wildlife park, Otter Sanctuary, play areas. Open all year, daily.

**Merlin's Magic Land**
Lelant, near Hayle. Tel: 01736 752885. Amusement park with rides. Open Apr–Oct, daily.

## Shopping

**Penzance**
Chapel Street has antiques and crafts shops. Main shopping area Market Jew Street and Causewayhead.

**St Ives**
Art galleries and crafts shops in the Fore Street area.

## LOCAL SPECIALITIES

**Crafts**
Gem and Jewellery Workshop, Pendeen. The Barbican, Wharf Road, Penzance. The Round House, Sennen. The Sloop, St Ives.

## The Performing Arts

**Acorn Theatre**
Parade Street, Penzance. Tel: 01736 365520. Excellent programme of theatre, music, arts.

**Minack Theatre**
Porthcurno. Open-air performances in summer only. Tel: 01736 810181.

## Sports, Activities and the Outdoors

### ANGLING

**Sea**
Trips available from St Ives, Penzance and Mousehole.

**Coarse**
Enquiries to South West Water. Tel: 01837 871565.

### BEACHES

**Carbis Bay**
Safe bathing, dogs not allowed.

**Hayle**
Hayle Towans; Mexico Towans, Upton Towans and Gwithian: Generally safe bathing. Surfing, lifeguards, dogs not allowed on part of Gwithian or on Hayle Towans.

**Marazion**
Wind-surfing, lifeguard, dogs not allowed.

**Penzance**
Long Rock Beach: shingle and sand, safe bathing. Dogs not allowed.

**Perranuthnoe**
Safe bathing, but sandbank may form at centre of beach.

**Porthcurno**
Safe bathing, but care needed during high tide. Lifeguard, dogs not allowed.

**Sennen**
Gwenver: spectacular surfing. Bathing between flags only; Sennen: Blue Flag Award, Seaside Award. Good surfing, safe bathing between flags only, lifeguard, dogs not allowed.

**St Ives**
Porthminster: safe bathing, lifeguard, dogs not allowed Easter–Sep; St Ives Harbour: sheltered, dogs not allowed Easter–Sep; Porthmeor: Blue Flag Award, Seaside Award, surfing beach, generally safe bathing, lifeguard, dogs not allowed Easter–Sep.

### BOAT TRIPS

**Penzance**
Isles of Scilly Steamship Company. Day trips to Isles of Scilly. Tel: O1736 334220/362009.

**St Ives**
Sea cruises from the harbour.

### BOWLING

**Penzance**
Bowling clubs at Penlee-Newlyn and St Ives. For details contact Tourist Information.

**Hayle**
West Cornwall Leisure and Bowling Club (Indoors) Queensway. Tel: 01736 752595.

### CYCLING

A network of quiet lanes offers good cycling between the main roads and main centres. Cycling is not permitted on public footpaths or on the coast path.

### CYCLE HIRE

**Hayle**
Hayle Cycles, 36 Penpol Terrace. Tel: 01736 753825.

**Penzance**
Bike Bitz, Albert Street. Tel: 01736 333243.
The Cycle Centre, Bread Street. Tel: 01736 351671.

### GOLF COURSES

**Lelant**
West Cornwall Golf Club. Tel: 01736 753401.

**St Ives**
Tregenna Castle. Tel: 01736 797381.

**St Just**
Cape Cornwall Golf Club. Tel: 01736 788611.

### HORSE-RIDING

**Lelant Downs**
Old Mill Stables. Tel: 01736 753045.

**St Ives**
Penhalwyn Trekking Centre, Halsetown. Tel: 01736 796461.

### PLEASURE FLIGHTS

Westward Airways, Land's End
Airport, St Just. Scenic flights.
Tel: 01736 788771.

### WATERSPORTS

**St Ives**
Wind and Sea, 25 Fore Street.
Tel: 01736 794830.
**Penzance**
Atlantic Aqua Sports, Albert
Street. Tel: 01736 365757.

## Annual Events and Customs

**Hayle**
Hayle Heritage Week. Jul–Aug.
**Newlyn**
Newlyn Fish Festival. August
Bank Holiday Mon.
**Penzance**
Golowan Festival and Mazey
Day. Two weeks mid-Jun,
ending on Saturday nearest
Midsummer's Day.
**St Ives**
St Ives Feast Day. Early Feb.
St Ives Festival of Music and the
Arts. First two weeks Sep.

## The Isles of Scilly

## Leisure Information

### TOURIST INFORMATION CENTRE

**St Mary's**
Wesleyan Chapel, Well Lane,
Hugh Town. Tel: 01720 422536.

### TRANSPORT

**Isles of Scilly Steamship
Company**
Quay Street, Penzance.
Tel: 01736 362009.
**British International
Helicopters**
The Heliport, Penzance.
Tel: 01736 363871.
**Isles of Scilly Skybus**
Land's End Airport, St Just,
Penzance. Tel: 01736 785220.

### ORDNANCE SURVEY MAPS

Explorer 1:25,000 Sheet 101
Landranger 1:50,000 Sheet 203
Outdoor Leisure 25 1:2500.

## Places of Interest

There will be an admission

charge at the following places
interest unless otherwise stated.
**ST MARY'S**
**Isles of Scilly Museum**
Church Street, Hugh Town.
Tel: 01720 422337. Open
Easter–Oct, Mon–Sat.
**Lifeboat House**
Hugh Town. Open all year.
**TRESCO**
**Abbey Garden and Valhalla**
Tel: 01720 422849. Open daily.
**Gallery Tresco**
New Grimsby. Tel: 01720
423105. Open Mon–Fri.

### BEACHES

**Bryher**
Several fine beaches, Rushy Bay
particularly good; sheltered,
south-facing, safe bathing.
**St Agnes**
Good, small beaches on the
south and east side of the island.
**St Martin's**
Good sun-traps on south coast.
Great Bay on north-east coast.
**St Mary's**
Hugh Town: Town Beach, on
harbour shore; Porthmellon
Beach, sandy. Dogs not allowed
May–Sep. Porthcressa Beach,
excellent, south-facing sandy
beach. Dogs not allowed
May–Sep. Old Town Bay: Sand,
rocks at low tide. Dogs not
allowed May–Sep. Porth Hellick:
Quiet bay, sand, but very rocky
and seaweed-covered at lowest
tide.
**Tresco**
Excellent sandy beaches at
Appletree Bay (south-west
coast), and at Rushy Point and
Pentle Bay (eastern coast).

*St Ives' Tate Gallery is a
work of art in itself*

## Sports, Activities and the Outdoors

### ANGLING

**Sea**
Trips from all main islands.

### BOAT TRIPS

**Bryher and Tresco**
Bryher Boat Services, Jenford.
Tel: 01720 422886.
**St Agnes**
St Agnes Boating. Tel: 01720
422704.
**St Mary's**
St Mary's Boatmen's Association,
Quayside.
**St Martin's**
St Martin's Boat Services.
Tel: 01720 422814.

### GOLF COURSE

Isles of Scilly Golf Club, St
Mary's. Tel: 01720 422692.

### GUIDED WALKS

Isles of Scilly Environmental
Trust, Hugh Town, St Mary's
Tel: 01720 422153.

### HORSE-RIDING

Three Horseshoes Riding Centre,
High Lanes, St Mary's.
Tel: 01720 422684.

### WATERSPORTS

**St Mary's**
Island Underwater Safaris,
Nowhere, Old Town. (Diving)
Tel: 01720 422732.
Isles of Scilly Underwater Centre,
Jackson Hill.
Tel: 01720 422595.
The Isles of Scilly Windsurf and
Sailing Centre, St Mary's Quay.
Tel: 01720 422037.
**St Martins'**
St Martin's Diving Centre,
Highertown. Tel: 01720 422848.

## Annual Events and Customs

### Gig racing

Events throughout the summer
from various points to St Mary's
Quay.
World Gig Racing
Championships early May.

# Atlas and Map Symbols

## THE NATIONAL GRID SYSTEM

The National Grid system covers Great Britain with an imaginary network of 100 kilometre grid squares. Each square is given a unique alphabetic reference as shown in the diagram. These squares are sub-divided into one hundred 10 kilometre squares, each numbered from 0 to 9 in an easterly (left to right) direction and northerly (upwards) direction from the bottom left corner. Each 10 km square is similarly sub-divided into one hundred 1 km squares.

Kilometres North

| | | | | | | | HP | |
| | | | | | HT | HU | | |
| | | | | | HY | HZ | | |
| NA | NB | NC | ND | NE | | | | |
| NF | NG | NH | NJ | NK | | | | |
| NL | NM | NN | NO | | | | | |
| NQ | NR | NS | NT | NU | | | | |
| | NW | NX | NY | NZ | | | | |
| | | SC | SD | SE | TA | | | |
| | | SH | SJ | SK | TF | TG | | |
| | | SM | SN | SO | SP | TL | TM | |
| | | SR | SS | ST | SU | TQ | TR | |
| | SV | SW | SX | SY | SZ | TV | | |

0   100   200   300   400   500   600   700
False Origin of National Grid
Kilometres East

## KEY TO ATLAS

MOTORWAY

M6

Service area

Service area (limited access)

Junction with junction number

Junction with limited interchange

Distance in miles between markers

Under construction

PRIMARY ROUTE

A34

Dual carriageway with service area

Primary route destination

YORK

Roundabout

Multiple level junction

Under construction

MAIN ROAD

A684

Dual carriageway

Road tunnel

Toll

Toll

Distance in miles between markers

8

SECONDARY ROAD

B6265

Dual carriageway

Gradient: 1 in 7 and steeper

Narrow road with passing places

Minor road

## KEY TO ATLAS

| ✝ | Abbey, Cathedral, Priory | | 🏎 | Motor racing |
| 🐟 | Aquarium | | 🏛 | Museum |
| ⊼ | Camp site | | ❗ | Nature or forest Trail |
| 🚐 | Caravan site | | 🦆 | Nature reserve |
| 🏰 | Castle | | ☆ | Other tourist features |
| | Cave | | ✕ | Picnic site |
| 🎪 | Country park | | 🚂 | Preserved railway |
| | Craft centre | | 🏇 | Racecourse |
| ❀ | Garden | | ⛷ | Skiing |
| ▶ | Golf course or links | | ☀ | Viewpoint |
| 🏛 | Historic house | | | Wildlife park |
| ℹ | Information centre | | 🐘 | Zoo |
| ✈ | Aerodrome with customs facilities | | ☎ | Motoring organisation telephone |
| ✈ | Aerodrome without customs facilities | | ☎ | Public telephone |
| Ⓗ | Heliport | | ⚲ | Radio or TV mast |
| | Lighthouse (in use and disused) | | 🌀 | Windmill |
| | Light-vessel | | | |

## KEY TO TOURS

| 🚗 | Tour start point | Buckland Abbey | Highlighted point of interest |
| ➡ | Direction of tour | | |
| ▪▪▶▪ | Optional detour | | Featured tour |

## KEY TO WALKS

Scale 1:25,000, 2½ inches to 1 mile, 4cm to 1 km

| | | | |
|---|---|---|---|
| 🚶🚶 | Start of walk | | Line of walk |
| ➡ | Direction of walk | ⊪▸▪▸ | Optional detour |
| | | Buckland Abbey | Highlighted point of interest |

## ROADS AND PATHS

| M1 or A6(M) | M1 or A6(M) | Motorway |
|---|---|---|
| A 31(T) or A35 | A 31(T) or A35 | Trunk or main road |
| B 3074 | B 3074 | Secondary road |
| A 35 | A 35 | Dual carriageway |
| | | Road generally more than 4m wide |
| | | Road generally less than 4m wide |
| | | Other road, drive or track |
| | | Path |

Unfenced roads and tracks are shown by pecked lines

## RAILWAYS

| | | |
|---|---|---|
| Multiple track Standard gauge | | Embankment |
| Single track | | Tunnel |
| Narrow gauge | | Road over; road under |
| Siding | | Level crossing |
| Cutting | | Station |

## PUBLIC RIGHTS OF WAY

Public rights of way may not be evident on the ground

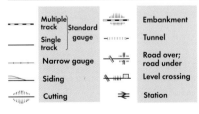

| | |
|---|---|
| Public paths { footpath bridleway | Byway open to all traffic |
| Permissive path | Road used as a public path |
| Permissive bridleway | Named path |
| Pennine Way | National trail or recreational path |

The representation on this map of any other road, track or path is no evidence of the existence of a right of way

## RELIEF

| 50 · | Heights determined by | Ground survey |
|---|---|---|
| 285 | | Air survey |

Contours are at 5 and 10 metres vertical interval

## SYMBOLS

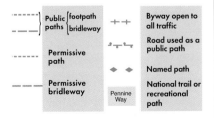

| | | | |
|---|---|---|---|
| Place of worship { with tower / with spire, minaret or dome / without such additions | | ○W, Spr | Well, Spring |
| | Building | | Gravel pit |
| | Important building | | Other pit or quarry |
| . T; A; R | Telephone: public; AA; RAC | | Sand pit |
| pylon pole | Electricity transmission line | | Refuse or slag heap |
| △ △ | Triangulation pillar | | County Boundary (England & Wales) |
| | Bus or coach station | | Water |
| | Lighthouse; beacon | | Sand; sand & shingle |
| | Site of antiquity | | National Park boundary |
| NT | National Trust always open | | Mud |
| FC | Forestry Commission | | |

## DANGER AREA

Firing and test ranges in the area
**Danger!**
Observe warning notices

## VEGETATION

Limits of vegetation are defined by positioning of the symbols but may be delineated also by pecks or dots

| | | | |
|---|---|---|---|
| | Coniferous trees | | Non-coniferous trees |
| | Orchard | | Heath |
| | Coppice | | Marsh, reeds, saltings. |

## TOURIST AND LEISURE INFORMATION

| | | | |
|---|---|---|---|
| △ | Camp site | PC | Public convenience |
| ℹ | Information centre | P | Parking |
| ℹ | Information centre (seasonal) | | Viewpoint |
| | Caravan site | ⊕ | Mountain rescue post |
| ⊽ | Picnic site | | |

Round Island
St Helen
White Island
St Martin's
Castle
New Tean
Grimsby
Higher Town
Bryher
Tresco
Samson
Eastern Isles
North West Passage
The Road
Crow Sound
HUGH TOWN
The Garrison
A3110
St Mary's
Crim Rocks
Broad Sound
St Mary's Sound
ISLES OF SCILLY
Annet
Gugh
Smith Sound
St Agnes
Western
Rocks

Padstow Bay
PADSTOW
Po
Constantine
Bay
A389
St Issey
Ro
Watergate
Bay
A392
St Mawgan
St Col
NEWQUAY
A392
A3059
46
3
Ligger or
Perran Bay
St Newlyn
East
St De
Perranporth
A3075
5
A305
ST-AU
St Agnes
13
A30
A39
Gramp
Porthtowan
17
A390
TRURO
Trego
Portreath
Fal
ST IVES
St Ives
Bay
28
St Day
REDRUTH
Veryan
A3074
11
CAMBORNE
A393
Feock
Ferry
A3078
Lelant
Hayle
PENRYN
Gerrans
Crowlas
6
Leedstown
10
A394
FALMOUTH
St Mawes
ST JUST
Marazion
FALMOUTH BAY
A3071
PENZANCE
A394
13
HELFORD RIVER
Whitesand Bay
30
13
Mawnan
A30
Newlyn
MOUNTS
BAY
HELSTON
Sennen
St Buryan
Mousehole
Mawgan
St Keverne
LAND'S END
B3315
Porthleven
Treen
Mullion
Coverack
A3083
Ruan Minor
Lizard
Wolf Rock
LIZARD POINT

Eddystone Rocks

0          20 km
0     10 miles

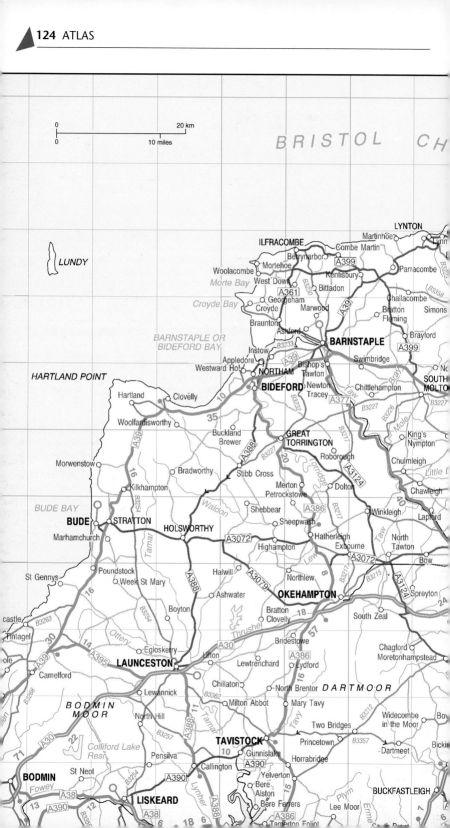

0        20 km
0      10 miles

BRISTOL  CH

LUNDY

LYNTON
Martinhoe
Lynn

ILFRACOMBE
Combe Martin
A399

Woolacombe    Mortehoe
West Down    Parracombe
Morte Bay    Berrynarbor
Croyde Bay    A361
Georgeham    Bittadon
Croyde    Marwood
Challacombe    Simons
Braunton    Bratton Fleming
Ashford    Brayford
BARNSTAPLE OR
BIDEFORD BAY    Instow    BARNSTAPLE    A399
Appledore    B3233    Swimbridge
Westward Ho!    Bishop's    No
NORTHAM    Tawton    SOUTH
HARTLAND POINT    BIDEFORD    Chittlehampton    MOLTO
Newton    A377
Hartland    Clovelly    Tracey    B3227    King's
Woolfardisworthy    Nympton
Buckland    GREAT    Chulmleigh
Brewer    TORRINGTON    Little
Morwenstow    Roborough    Chawleigh
Bradworthy    A3124
Stibb Cross    Dolton    Lapford
Kilkhampton    Merton    A386    Winkleigh    North
Petrockstowe    Tawton
BUDE BAY    Shebbear    Sheepwash    Bow
BUDE    STRATTON    Hatherleigh    A3072
Marhamchurch    HOLSWORTHY    A3072    Exbourne    A3124
Highampton    Spreyton
St Gennys    Poundstock    Halwill    Northlew    OKEHAMPTON
Week St Mary    Ashwater    South Zeal
castle    B3263    Boyton    Bratton    Chagford
Tintagel    Clovelly    Moretonhampstead
ole    Egloskerry    A30    Bridestowe    A386
Camelford    Lifton    Lewtrenchard    Lydford
LAUNCESTON    Chillaton    DARTMOOR
Lewannick    North Brentor
BODMIN    North Hill    Milton Abbot    Mary Tavy
MOOR    Widecombe    Bo
Colliford Lake    Two Bridges    in the Moor
Resr    Pensilva    TAVISTOCK    Princetown    Dartmeet    Bicki
BODMIN    St Neot    Gunnislake    A390    Horrabridge
Callington    Yelverton
LISKEARD    A390    Bere    BUCKFASTLEIGH
A38    Alston
Bere Ferrers
Lee Moor
Tamerton Foliot

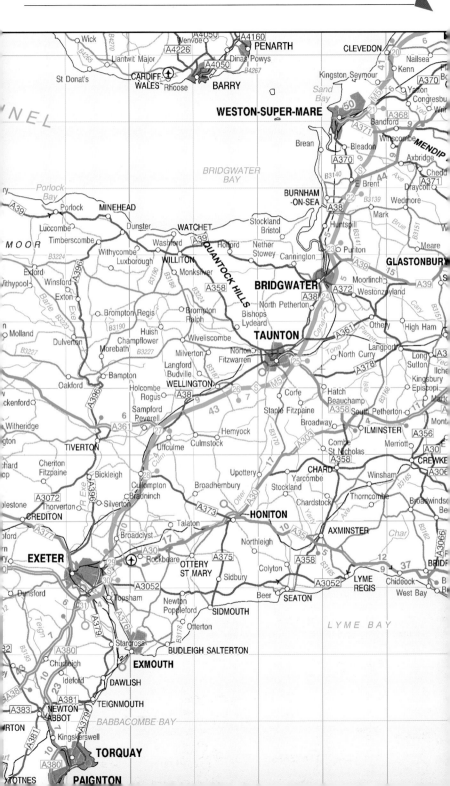

# Index

# *Acknowledgements*

The author would like to thank the Tourism Departments of Restormel, North Cornwall, Caradon, Carrick, Kerrier and Penwith District Councils, The Isles of Scilly Tourist Board, the Cornwall Tourist Board and the National Trust In Cornwall, for their invaluable assistance.

The Automobile Association would like to thank the following photographers and libraries for their assistance in the preparation of this book.

MARY EVANS PICTURE LIBRARY 6e, 7f
THE MANSELL COLLECTION LTD 6a, 7a
ROGER MOSS 115, 116
NATURE PHOTOGRAPHERS LTD 7c (A Cleeve)

The remaining pictures are held in the Association's own library (AA PHOTO LIBRARY) and were taken by Roger Moss with the exception of page 29 which was taken by P Baker, pages 3j, 7d, 7e, 12b which were taken by A Lawson and pages 11a, 17, 18 taken by N Ray